BLACK ✦ STARS

AFRICAN AMERICAN RELIGIOUS LEADERS

✦

JIM HASKINS AND KATHLEEN BENSON

WILEY

John Wiley & Sons, Inc.

© 2008 by Jim Haskins and Kathleen Benson. All rights reserved.

Published by Jossey-Bass
A Wiley Imprint
989 Market Street, San Francisco, CA 94103-1741
www.josseybass.com

Jossey-Bass books and products are available through most bookstores. To contact Jossey-Bass directly call our Customer Care Department within the U.S. at 800-956-7739, outside the U.S. at 317-572-3986, or fax 317-572-4002.

Jossey-Bass also publishes its books in a variety of electronic formats. Some content that appears in print may not be available in electronic books.

Library of Congress Cataloging-in-Publication Data

Haskins, James, 1941–2005
    African American religious leaders / Jim Haskins and Kathleen Benson. — 1st ed.
        p. cm. — (Black stars)
    Includes bibliographical references and index.
    ISBN 978-0-471-73632-5 (cloth: alk. paper)
    1. Christian leadership. 2. African American leadership. 3. Christian biography. 4. African Americans—Biography. I. Benson, Kathleen. II. Title.
BV652.1.H285 2007
277.3'08092396073—dc22
[B]   2007027347

Printed in the United States of America
first edition

10 9 8 7 6 5 4 3 2 1

In memory of Jim Haskins and his brother, Eddie Haskins

ACKNOWLEDGMENTS

This book was conceived by Jim Haskins, who passed away before we had finished researching the lives of the leaders to be included. Jim sought the assistance of Bernice Cosey Pulley, a graduate of Yale Divinity School and founder of Church Women United, Waterside–United Nations Unit. She was very helpful in compiling the list of leaders. Jim would also have acknowledged the support of John Weber, whose Welcome Rain publishing company issued *Keeping the Faith: African American Sermons of Liberation* (2001), a collection of sermons by contemporary religious leaders that Jim compiled and edited. I am grateful to Kate Bradford, editor at John Wiley, for giving me the opportunity to complete the project, and to the artist, photographer, and historian Betsy Braun Lane for suggesting that Maria Stewart be included among the African American religious leaders profiled here. Our conversations led me to include more women religious leaders than originally planned.

CONTENTS

INTRODUCTION

✦

Throughout the history of Africans in America, no need has been greater than the need to believe that there is a purpose to life and that others share the same belief. Religion meets that need, and it is not surprising that religion has been one of the most powerful forces in African American life since Africans first arrived as slaves on North American shores.

The Atlantic slave trade threw together Africans of many different languages and cultures and forced them to live, work, and communicate with one another. They were prevented from keeping their native religions and either encouraged or compelled to adopt Christianity. Treated as one people, they eventually became one people. By the time of the Revolutionary War, people of African heritage had been in America for one hundred fifty years and had created a strong sense of group identity.

The core around which black people coalesced was religion. Whether enslaved or free—and by the time of the Revolution there was a substantial population of free blacks in the North—black people looked to the spirit of hope bestowed by the belief in a higher power and took advantage of the opportunities to find community that religious services provided.

In the years between the turn of the nineteenth century and the Civil War, the growing community consciousness among black people continued. Black people formed more institutions, and more black leaders arose from the community. The two largest African American religious denominations, the African Methodist Episcopal Church, founded in 1816, and the African Methodist Episcopal Zion Church, founded in the early 1820s, extended their reach and centralized their organizations.

The Civil War ended legal slavery. During a period after the war called Reconstruction, Federal troops oversaw the creation of new governments in the former Confederate states, started schools, and gave other help to the freed people of the South. The post–Civil War Reconstruction period was also an era of institution building for African Americans. A third black Methodist denomination, the Colored Methodist Episcopal Church, was established in the South during this time. The Baptist Church, slower to organize nationally than the other Protestant denominations, finally formed the National Baptist Convention for its black churches in 1895.

The promise of freedom proved elusive for black people in the South. After Reconstruction ended, new southern segregation laws effectively reduced African Americans to virtual slavery. Religion and the organized churches became an even more important source of solace and community. After World War I ended in 1919, many southern black people moved to northern cities to find jobs and escape the violence and intimidation of segregation. They found a sense of power in their great numbers, and the influence of black churches grew.

Black religious leaders had varying ideas about how to challenge racial injustice in America—or whether to challenge it at all—but by the time World War II ended in 1945, the majority agreed that the black church not only had to be a center of community life but also had to be involved in political matters. Some leaders went so far as to campaign for elective office, using their churches as a political base. Others used their moral influence and their large followings to mount a campaign for equal rights. It is no accident that most major leaders of the civil rights movement of the 1950s and 1960s were black ministers.

The religious leaders of the baby boom (those born between 1946 and 1955) missed the direct-action civil rights movement of the 1950s and 1960s. They did not have the opportunity to join together with other religious leaders in a fight that was so clearly about justice versus injustice. The civil rights movement had a well-defined goal: national legislation that would legally end segregation and voting discrimination. It is impossible to legislate attitudes. Some religious leaders of the baby boom generation have continued to use the tactics of the civil rights movement, but most have not. The majority have used the greater opportunities available to African Americans in the late twentieth and early twenty-first centuries to help their people—not only those who are impoverished and poorly educated, but also those who have been successful yet miss the sense of community that the black church has provided over the centuries. Today's leaders have learned to use the mass communication and technology tools of the late twentieth and early twenty-first centuries in their religious work. They are men and women grappling with the challenges of their time.

This history of African American religious leaders starts in the time of slavery and highlights some of the most important leaders in each era through the present day. In the first chapters of this book, nearly all the important leaders of their time are discussed. As time marched on, more and more religious leaders arose, so in later chapters of the book, only some of the most important leaders are profiled. They were chosen because they represented major trends, were firsts in their fields, or accomplished something unique. Most achieved their leadership positions against great odds.

PART ONE

✦

LEADERS OF THE REVOLUTIONARY ERA

ABSALOM
JONES

(1746–1818)

and

RICHARD
ALLEN

(1760–1831)

✦

African American clergymen in the Revolutionary era used the pulpit as a platform to fight for their people. Two of the first were Absalom Jones and Richard Allen, who were born into slavery fourteen years apart. They met in Philadelphia, Pennsylvania, where they founded one of the most important black churches, the African Methodist Episcopal (AME) Church.

Absalom Jones was born in Delaware in 1746. Portraits of him as an adult depict a heavyset man with small eyes and a long upper lip that make his mouth appear downturned and stern, but it is hard to tell from such images just what a person looked like when he was not sitting and posing for a portrait painter. As a youth, Jones worked as a servant in the home of his owner, where he had access to his owner's books. He taught himself to read by studying the New Testament of the Bible. When he was sixteen, his owner sold him to a merchant in Philadelphia named Wynkoop.

The city of Philadelphia and the surrounding colony of Pennsylvania had been founded by Quakers. This religious sect began in England in the 1600s as the Society of Friends, with the main belief that "God is within us." The ability to feel God caused some early members of the Society of Friends to shiver or quake, which earned them the nickname "Quakers." Although there were Quaker slave owners in Pennsylvania, Quakers were generally against slavery. Absalom Jones was able to continue his education at a night school for black people operated by Quakers.

Jones attended St. Peter's Anglican Church in Philadelphia. The congregation was predominantly white, but slave parishioners were treated with some sense of their humanity. Jones was twenty-three when he married a fellow slave named Mary in the church on January 4, 1770.

Under Pennsylvania law, children inherited the legal status of their mother, which meant that any children born to Mary while she remained in slavery would also be slaves. Neither Absalom Jones nor his bride wanted their children born in slavery, so the couple set about earning enough money to purchase Mary's freedom. When they could not save enough, Jones appealed to everyone he knew for loans. He composed and circulated a written appeal. In a city with many citizens who were against slavery, he managed to collect enough money to buy his wife's freedom from her owner. Jones then set about earning the money to pay back the debt. It took him until 1778 to do so, working by day for his owner and by night for himself and his family.

Jones would have liked to purchase his own freedom, but Wynkoop did not want to give up his slave. During that time, the Revolutionary War broke out, and there were many opportunities for work. Jones's owner allowed him to hire himself out to other employers. He eventually saved enough to buy a house and a lot in the southern part of the city. Finally, in 1784, Wynkoop agreed to allow Jones to purchase his own freedom.

Richard Allen was also born a slave, in Philadelphia in 1760. Of the six or seven paintings and drawings made of him as an adult, most depict a light-skinned man with slightly raised eyebrows—as if he were always questioning. He and his family were later sold to a farmer in Delaware. In 1777, when he was seventeen years old, Allen met a traveling black preacher, Freeborn Garretson, who was carrying word of a new church, the Methodist Episcopal Church.

An offshoot of the Anglican Church, or Church of England, the Methodist Episcopal Church did not recognize the same class distinctions as the older church. It had great appeal to slaves because it preached that slaveholders would be punished on Judgment Day. Meetings and services were more emotional and demonstrative than in the Anglican Church, with many more opportunities for participation by parishioners. It was very common for members of the congregation to testify to their faith or recall how they had come to the church. The church also taught that women were equal in the eyes of God. Not surprisingly, many early church leaders were women.

Under Freeborn Garretson's influence, Richard Allen's owner had a change of heart about being a slave owner. He did not free Allen outright, but he allowed Allen to earn enough money by sawing wood and driving a wagon to eventually buy his freedom.

After the Revolutionary War, Allen became a "licensed exhorter" in the Methodist Episcopal Church, which meant that he had the official sanction of the church to travel around preaching and gaining converts. He was so successful that he attracted the attention of church leaders. In 1786, he was appointed an assistant minister of the racially mixed congregation of St. George's Methodist Church in Philadelphia.

By that time, Absalom Jones had also responded to the preaching of the Methodist Church and had joined St. George's, where he was a lay, or unordained, minister to the black members of the congregation. Allen and Jones became friends. Together, they greatly increased the membership of St. George's—so much so, in fact, that the white parishioners began to feel threatened. Without informing the black parishioners, the church administrators decided to segregate them in an upstairs gallery. Shocked and angered, Jones, Allen, and their fellow black congregants refused to be segregated. The following Sunday, they took their places as usual on the main floor of the church, and when ushers attempted to remove them, the entire black congregation walked out.

Jones and Allen wanted to form their own religious group, but they soon discovered it would be difficult. The free black population of Philadelphia was small and attended many different churches. Also, there was opposition from both blacks and whites to the idea of a separate church. So, in 1787, Jones and Allen formed a nondenominational mutual aid society. They called it the Free African Society in a testament to the strong ties they still felt to Africa. The Free African Society was the first organization of free black people to be formed in the United States, and it had many aims. Its primary purpose was to act independently of whites and for the good of its membership. The Free African Society charged membership dues, and its rules provided for those funds to be used for the welfare of members who needed it, or for the widows and children of members who died.

Jones and Allen continued to feel that they needed a church, and eventually they set about raising the money to build a structure. Disagreements over religious practices led to a split in the congregation, however. The strong Quaker influence in Philadelphia religious life led a majority of those in the Free African Society to adopt the Quaker practice of having fifteen minutes of silence at meetings. Those who preferred the more expressive practices of Methodism objected, and in 1789, Richard Allen led a group that withdrew from the Free African Society. Under the leadership of Absalom Jones, the Free African Society continued its fundraising efforts and broke ground for a new church building in 1792.

In 1793, Jones, Allen, and others among the free black population of Philadelphia put their differences aside and joined in the common cause of helping their fellow inhabitants of the city during the largest yellow fever epidemic in American history. It killed some five thousand people, or about 10 percent of the city's population.

Absalom Jones presided over the dedication of St. Thomas African Episcopal Church on July 17, 1794. The new church then applied for membership in the Episcopal Diocese of Pennsylvania under the following conditions: (1) that they be recognized as an organized body; (2) that they have control over their local affairs; (3) that Absalom Jones be licensed as a lay reader, and, if qualified, be ordained as minister. In October 1794, the church was admitted to the diocese as St. Thomas African Episcopal Church, and in 1795, Bishop White ordained Jones as deacon. Seven years later, on September 21, 1802, Jones was the first black American to receive formal ordination as a priest.

Richard Allen, meanwhile, led those who had withdrawn from the African Episcopal Church and formed a Methodist congregation, the Bethel African Methodist Episcopal Church. It opened in July 1794, the same month in which St. Thomas African Episcopal Church was dedicated. Although that ceremony was presided over by the white Methodist bishop Francis Asbury, Allen and his fellow congregants were determined to worship separately from whites. They wanted to control their own religious lives, to allow those with a deep faith and oratorical skills to preach without seeking permission from higher church authorities. Bishop Asbury ordained Richard Allen in 1799, and his powerful preaching attracted an ever-growing congregation.

Philadelphia's black population burgeoned after the Revolutionary War, and the Bethel AME congregation grew quickly. Richard Allen understood that the community needed to be educated, and he opened a day school in 1795. In 1804, he established the Society of Free People of Colour for Promoting the Instruction and School Education of Children of African Descent.

Two years later, Allen was seized as a fugitive slave. Under the Fugitive Slave Act of 1793, which allowed slave owners to travel to the North to reclaim enslaved people who had run away, any person of color was fair game. Allen was able to prove that he had purchased his own freedom many years before. But the fact that a man of Allen's stature could be subject to seizure was proof that as long as slavery existed in the United States, no black person was safe. The experience made him even more determined to separate himself and his followers from whites.

Efforts by Methodist church authorities to curb the church's black congregations fueled Allen's determination. Bethel won legal recognition as an independent church in 1816. That same year, Allen and representatives from black Methodist congregations in Baltimore, Maryland; Wilmington, Delaware; Salem, New Jersey; and Attleboro, Pennsylvania, met at Bethel Church to organize a new denomination, the African Methodist Episcopal (AME) Church, as the first completely independent black denomination in America. This convocation chose Richard Allen as the first bishop of the new church, acknowledging his role in creating a separate religious identity for his people. He became the second black American to be formally ordained, after his friend Absalom Jones.

Some white Philadelphians feared the power of the new black church. In 1818, white authorities disrupted an AME service and arrested one hundred forty people. But the strong tradition of equality in the city founded by Quakers prevailed, and the AME Church flourished there and spread to other northern cities.

Absalom Jones died in 1818. Richard Allen lived for thirteen years after the death of his friend. During that time, a movement to resettle African Americans in the Republic of Haiti arose. Slaves in the former French colony had revolted in 1804 and declared Haiti an independent republic. As the ideals of equality expressed in the Constitution of the new United States of America seemed more and more elusive for black people, many African Americans began to envision a future of freedom in Haiti. The Haitian Emigration Society was formed in 1824 to help African Americans settle there, and Richard Allen supported it. But after that effort failed, Allen decided that emigration was not a realistic option. He urged his fellow African Americans to remain in the United States. In 1827, he wrote in *Freedom's Journal*, the first black newspaper, "This land which we have watered with our tears and our blood is now our mother country."[1]

JARENA COX LEE (1783–?)

The Reverend Richard Allen gave Jarena Cox Lee the opportunity to be the first woman authorized to preach in the AME Church. Jarena Cox was born to free parents in Cape May, New Jersey, but they were so poor that they could not take care of her. She was sent to live and work in the homes of strangers when she was seven years old.

In 1811, Jarena Cox married Joseph Lee, who was pastor of a church in a small town outside Philadelphia. Upon hearing a sermon by the Reverend Richard Allen, founder of the AME Church, she was so inspired that she decided she wanted to preach the gospel. She asked Allen for permission, but he denied her, explaining that it was considered unseemly for women to speak in public.

Jarena Lee was only able to use her newfound sense of mission within the confines of her small-town church community. After she gave birth to two children, she was kept busy with wife- and motherhood. Then her husband died, leaving her a widow and her children fatherless. She turned to her religion for solace.

Later, the Reverend Richard Allen happened to be present at a meeting presided over by a visiting minister where Jarena Lee was the preacher. He was so impressed with Jarena Lee's exhortations to God that he changed his mind about letting her preach. In fact, he stood up during the service and confessed that he should have let her preach when she had asked him eight years earlier.

Being a woman, Jarena Lee could not possibly have a church of her own. So, she became an itinerant preacher, traveling thousands of miles, sometimes even into dangerous slave-holding towns. In one year alone, she recorded in her journal that she traveled 2,335 miles and preached 178 sermons. She recorded a number of conversions, including conversions of slave owners.

In 1833, Jarena Lee began working with an editor to turn her religious journal into an autobiography. *Religious Experience and Journal of Mrs. Jarena Lee* was published in 1836, and she published two more editions in 1839 and 1849. It is not known what became of Jarena Lee after 1849.

L E M U E L

HAYNES

(1753–1833)

✦

Lemuel Haynes was born in West Hartford, Connecticut. He spent his entire life in New England, where the population of black people was minuscule. His African father was among the few black men in West Hartford. His mother was a white woman who abandoned him at birth. As was the case with orphans of any race at the time, he was indentured, or bound to service, until he was twenty-one. Haynes's employer was a man named Hadley in Middle Granville, Massachusetts.

Haynes did not receive much education while he was with Hadley, but he did learn to read and write. Allowed to read the Bible and to attend the local Congregational church, Haynes developed a deep faith. He was still a teenager when he began conducting services at his church and even delivered sermons he had written. Light-complexioned, with heavy black eyebrows and a bulbous nose, he had great strength of character and drew people to him through his religious convictions.

Haynes's term of service to Hadley ended in 1774. War between Great Britain and her American colonies was brewing, and Haynes joined the Minutemen, the nickname for the local militia, which signified that they would be ready in a minute to defend their towns.

Around 1776, Haynes wrote a manuscript in which he stated "that an African . . . has an undeniable right to his Liberty."[1] He also called slavery a sin and wrote that it was ironic that slave owners should fight for their own liberty while denying it to others. But he never published that manuscript, and in fact, it was not discovered until he had been dead for one hundred fifty years.

After the Revolutionary War ended, Haynes studied for the ministry. Licensed to preach in 1780, he was ordained as a Congregationalist minister in 1785. He was hired as pastor of an all-white church in Torrington, Connecticut, but left after two years because of the racism of some of its members. He served as pastor of a white congregation in Rutland, Vermont, for some thirty years, although he and his wife encountered prejudice there as well and eventually left. After serving as minister of a church in Manchester, Vermont, for a time, Haynes took his last position as a minister in upstate New York, where he died in 1833 at the age of eighty.

Haynes was a gifted preacher and writer. In fact, he achieved an international reputation for his sermons and writings and was honored for both. He received an honorary master of arts degree from Middlebury College, the first such degree to be given to a black person. He believed deeply in the equality of all men before God, but he chose not to be an activist preacher. His situation as a biracial minister in a historically white church in an almost exclusively white society gave him little opportunity to share his true feelings.

Had Haynes lived in a different place—in Philadelphia or Boston, for example, where he could have joined with other black leaders—he might have made a difference for his fellow African Americans. As it was, he could only show by his own example what a person with African blood was capable of achieving.

PETER WILLIAMS SR. (1749–1823)

Peter Williams Sr. was born into slavery. Williams's owner attended John Street Methodist Church in New York City, and as an adult, Williams went to work there as a sexton, or custodian. As the colonies became increasingly restive under British rule, Williams's owner, who was a Loyalist (someone who remained loyal to Britain), decided to leave the colonies and return to England. But he could not take Williams with him because slavery had been outlawed in Great Britain in 1770. The congregation of John Street Methodist Church decided to purchase Williams's freedom.

PETER WILLIAMS JR. (1780–1840)

Williams's son, Peter Williams Jr., was born in 1780 in New Brunswick, New Jersey. The younger Williams was sixteen years old in 1796 when his father led a walkout of the black parishioners from John Street Methodist Church. Tired of being discriminated against by the white church hierarchy and white parishioners, the group formed the first black denomination in New York City, the African Methodist Episcopal Zion Church. AME Zion was chartered by the Episcopal Diocese of America in 1801.

Peter Jr. became very active in the AME Zion Church. In 1818, he organized the first African American Episcopal parish in New York, St. Philip's African Church on Centre Street. Eight years later, he was ordained as the first black Episcopal priest. The following year, he helped to found *Freedom's Journal*, the first black newspaper in the United States.

J O H N
MARRANT

(1755–1791)

◆

J ohn Marrant was born to a free black family in New York City. His
father died when he was four, and his mother moved the family around
for several years. Eventually, the family settled in Charleston, South
Carolina, where eleven-year-old John decided to study music. He
learned to play the French horn and violin, and by the time he was thirteen, he was in great demand to play at dances and parties.

One evening, on a dare, Marrant entered a local Methodist church,
intent upon blowing his French horn and disrupting the sermon. Instead,
he found himself struck as if by lightning by the power of the preacher,
the white evangelist George Whitefield. He decided then and there to
join the Methodist Church.

Marrant found no support at home for his newfound faith, and eventually he left home and family disapproval behind. As he related the

story, he wandered in the wilderness until he was found by a Cherokee hunter. The hunter took him back to his village, but the people there regarded Marrant as a stranger and a spy and decided to put him to death. The hunter pleaded for Marrant's life to no avail, and it was John Marrant who saved his own life. He did so, he reported years later, through prayer. The Cherokee were struck by his deep faith and his mesmerizing prayers and decided to spare him. Marrant claimed to have converted several of the village inhabitants to Methodism and to have found a new calling. He spent two years living among the Cherokee and other Native American peoples. When he returned home in Native American dress, his family didn't even recognize him. They had given up hope that they would ever see him again.

By the time Marrant returned home, the Revolutionary War was in progress. Marrant served in the South Carolina navy. Upon his discharge in the early 1780s, he met evangelist George Whitefield again and renewed his commitment to God. He was ordained in the Methodist Church in 1785 and that same year published his autobiography in pamphlet form. It proved to be very popular and was reprinted several times.

John's brother was living in Nova Scotia, where many free black people and fugitive slaves had settled. He urged John in a letter to join him and preach Methodism there. With money and blessings from a British Methodist woman named Huntingdon, Marrant traveled to the free black town of Birchtown, Nova Scotia. He started a church, ministering to the small black colony and the much larger Native American population.

Marrant labored in a wilderness, traveling around and preaching to isolated settlements. He suffered constantly from exposure to the elements, hunger, and exhaustion. He wrote in his journal, "In my greatest illness my chief diet was fish and potatoes, and sometimes a little tea sweetened with treacle, and this was the best they could afford, and the bed whereon I laid was stuffed with straw, with two blankets, without sheets; and this was reckoned a very great advantage in these parts of the globe; for in some places I was obliged to lay on stools, without any blanket, when the snow was five and six feet on the earth, and sometimes in a cave on the earth itself."[1]

During a smallpox epidemic in 1787, he was bedridden for more than a week. That same year, the region was hit by a famine.

Marrant had spent more than three years in Nova Scotia when he was called to return to the United States by the leaders of the branch of Methodism he favored. His orders were to go to Boston to preach, so he boarded a ship bound for Boston on January 27, 1788. He never returned to Nova Scotia, but he recorded his experiences there in his journal, which was published in 1790 under the title *Journal of the Reverend John Marrant*.

Having lived for several years free of slavery and open racial discrimination, Marrant returned to the country of his birth a changed man. He joined the Prince Hall Grand Lodge, Free and Accepted Masons. This all-black lodge, established just after the Revolutionary War by a black man named Prince Hall, actively campaigned for the abolition of slavery.

Marrant believed that black people could only be truly free outside the United States, and he decided to lead an expedition to Sierra Leone on the west coast of Africa, a colony that Great Britain had established for its former slaves after outlawing slavery. This plan was not part of the mission that his benefactor, Huntingdon, had had in mind for him, however. Before Marrant could complete his preparations for the Sierra Leone trip, he was summoned to England to explain why he had failed to use the money given to him in support of his original mission. He traveled to London in March 1790. Not long after he arrived, his health began to fail. A combination of old war wounds suffered while he served in the South Carolina navy during the Revolutionary War, the effects of his bout with smallpox, and the hardships of life as a traveling preacher had aged him far beyond his thirty-five years. He stayed in London and preached at a small church in a suburb of London called Islington. He died in 1791 and was buried in the cemetery of the small church where he had preached his last sermons.

Thus far, all the religious leaders we have discussed lived in the North. Conditions in the South did not encourage black leadership, at least of the public, documented kind. Unlike the North, which had a comparatively small number of black people, whether enslaved or free, the South had a huge slave population. In fact, in some parts of the region, black people far outnumbered white people. As a result, many whites lived in fear of slave uprisings, so almost all gatherings of Africans were suspect. From time to time and especially after slave revolts, Southerners passed laws stating that black people could not congregate together in numbers greater than three. Any slave who demonstrated leadership was immediately regarded as a potential revolt leader. Under such circumstances, only a small number of public leaders emerged.

Denmark Vesey was one of the few. He was born on the island of St. Thomas in the British Virgin Islands. He was probably named simply Denmark at birth—few slaves had last names. In 1771, when Denmark was fourteen years old, he was sold to Captain Joseph Vesey, a slave trader, and transported along with other slaves to the South Carolina port of Cape Français. There, Vesey sold Denmark to another man. Denmark was not happy about this turn of events. He pretended to have seizures, causing his new owner to believe he was not fit to work.

The next time Captain Vesey returned to Cape Français, Denmark's new owner insisted on returning his slave and getting his money back. Deciding that he could not resell Denmark, Captain Vesey kept the young slave with him, putting him to work on his ship. Denmark evidently liked Captain Vesey. He recovered his health immediately. Denmark took "Vesey" for his own last name and remained with Captain Vesey until the captain retired and settled in Charleston.

In Charleston, Denmark met and married an enslaved woman. Their children were also slaves, the property of the woman's owner. The entire family might have remained enslaved for life if Denmark Vesey had not been lucky as well as clever. In 1799, he won $600 in a lottery and was able to purchase his freedom. He probably chose to purchase himself rather than his wife so that he could then work to buy her freedom and subsequently that of his children.

Vesey attended Second Presbyterian Church, sitting in a special section reserved for slaves, or perhaps attending separate services. He did not leave the Presbyterian Church when a Methodist church was started in Charleston, but he knew many enslaved people who did. He was impressed when he learned that the black Methodists had started a secret freedom fund and was angered when whites found out about it and put an end to the plan. Fearing that other things were being plotted in secret, white residents of Charleston began to restrict the activity of blacks at the white churches. The final straw came when the black people of Charleston learned of plans by the Charleston Bethel Church to build a shed for hearses on an African burial ground. In a protest around 1815, black residents of Charleston left the white churches.

By this time, the African Methodist Episcopal Church, formed by Richard Allen and others in Philadelphia in the middle 1790s, was twenty years old and had spread to many northern cities. The black residents of Charleston formed their own AME Church, and in 1817, Denmark Vesey left the Presbyterian Church to join them. They didn't have money to buy or build a church structure, so they held services in their homes. Vesey became a lay preacher, or "class leader," presiding over services for small groups in his home.

The white residents of Charleston did not like the idea of a black church at all and made every effort to disrupt its services and arrest its leaders. Vesey became increasingly angry at this interference. He started teaching from the Old Testament of the Bible, especially from the book of Exodus, which dealt with the efforts of the Israelites to escape slavery. He taught his listeners that they were the New Israelites, a chosen people, and that God would punish those who had enslaved them. He preached what would later be called a theology of liberation.

This talk was dangerous, especially at a time when southern slave owners were worried about increasing efforts to erode slavery in the United States. Slavery was a constant sticking point in relations between northern and southern states. Every time a new state was admitted to the Union, the biggest concern was whether it should be a slave state or free. In 1820, under the Missouri Compromise, Missouri entered the Union as a free state and Maine as a slave state. The United States was then made up of twenty-four states, half slave and half free. Those who wanted to abolish slavery altogether believed that they could soon tip the balance against slavery and eventually outlaw it in the nation. Many of the pro-slavery forces were determined to protect the institution of slavery at any cost. In some slave-holding areas, a wave of hysteria gripped the white populace.

In Charleston, rumors began to circulate of a plot by slaves to rise up against the city's whites, kill as many as possible, and then escape by ship to Haiti, the only independent black nation in the Western Hemisphere. Haiti had been formed as a result of a slave revolution on the French colony of Saint-Domingue in 1791. The Charleston plotters were using the black churches as their base, holding services as covers for meetings and church networks to spread the word. The date of the planned revolt in Charleston was said to be July 14, 1822.

On June 22, 1822, Denmark Vesey was arrested as one of the conspirators. Eventually, a total of 131 slaves would be charged. In the trial that followed, 33 slaves, after being beaten and threatened with execution, testified about the details of the plot. Denmark Vesey did not say a word. He refused to admit to any kind of plot or to speak against his fellows. Sixty-seven were convicted, and eventually thirty-five were executed. It was the largest number of executions ever carried out by a civilian court.

Denmark Vesey met his death by hanging on July 2, 1822. The official report of the trial court named Vesey as the head of the conspiracy. Over time, as the idea of slavery became repugnant to the majority of Americans, Vesey was hailed as a heroic freedom fighter.

One hundred eighty years after Vesey's death, a historian at Johns Hopkins University named Michael Johnson decided to read the transcript of the trial proceedings and found a different story. Johnson concluded that there was never a plot to revolt, that frightened slave holders—incited by the mayor of Charleston, who used the supposed plot as a means to advance his own career—had concocted the story and coerced false testimony from a handful of scared slaves and free blacks who had probably been threatened with execution if they did not testify. Johnson found no evidence that Denmark Vesey had even testified in court. The so-called official report was a fabrication; that is, what had seemed to be a conspiracy on the part of slaves and freed blacks to revolt against whites was in fact a conspiracy on the part of whites to get rid of or frighten outspoken black slaves and freemen.

Although not every historian has accepted this radically different view of the events in Charleston in 1822, some of the most respected historians have done so. It will take a long time to put to rest the myth of the Vesey revolt.

After the trial and the executions, white residents of Charleston took further steps to ensure that no future plot would ever be hatched under the cloak of religion. They burned down homes suspected of hosting services of the AME Church and passed laws restricting meetings of slaves. Denmark Vesey's family was not safe in Charleston. His wife, Susan, emigrated to Liberia, a settlement for free black people established on the west coast of Africa by the American Colonization Society. One of his sons went to Cuba. Another son, Robert, helped to rebuild the AME Church in Charleston some forty years later, in 1865.

Even if Denmark Vesey did not plan a revolt, he continues to be regarded as a hero, along with the others who refused to give false testimony even when faced with torture and death. There were also white heroes—twenty-seven Charleston whites who testified in support of some of the black defendants. Before Michael Johnson exposed the white conspiracy, the City of Charleston was planning a monument to Vesey as a revolutionary. Plans for the monument moved forward because the true story was also a story of quiet heroism.

PART TWO

✦

LEADERS OF THE CIVIL WAR ERA

I Sell the Shadow to Support the Substance.
SOJOURNER TRUTH.

SOJOURNER
TRUTH

(1797?–1883)

◆

The woman who later named herself Sojourner Truth was born in Ulster County in upstate New York, an area that had been settled by Dutch immigrants in the 1600s. Her given name was Isabella. The Dutch influence was so strong that in her early years Isabella spoke only the Dutch language. Her parents were Elizabeth (Betsey) and James. Her father was very tall and straight, and as a young man he was given the name of Baumfree (also spelled Bomefree), which is the Dutch word for "tree." The Baumfree family were slaves on the estate of Colonel Johannes Hardenbergh.

Isabella was one of ten or twelve children. Telling the story of her life after she had grown up, Isabella said she could not remember how many siblings she had, because she was next to youngest, and all her older brothers and sisters had been sold away from the family by the time she was old enough to understand the circumstances. Among her earliest memories was listening to her parents mourn the sale of the two children who had been born before her—a boy of five and a girl of three.

Isabella's mother was deeply religious, and she taught her remaining children to believe that there was a higher power. At night, when the day's work was done, she would gather Isabella and her younger brother Peter to tell them about God. Years later, Isabella remembered her mother saying, "My children, there is a God, who hears and sees you. . . . He lives in the sky, and when you are beaten, or cruelly treated, or fall into any trouble, you must ask help of him, and he will always hear and help you."[1]

When Colonel Hardenbergh died, a relative named Charles Hardenbergh took over the estate. After Charles Hardenbergh died in 1808, his property, including slaves, was put up for auction. The auction notice advertised "slaves, horses, and other cattle." Isabella, who was about nine, was sold to a man named Nealy, who paid $100 for her and a herd of sheep.

Nealy and his family treated Isabella cruelly, frequently beating her when she did not immediately obey them. Part of the problem was that she did not understand English, so she learned quickly in a vain effort to avoid being beaten. Through all her hardships, Isabella never lost faith. In fact, she was certain that she could have avoided the beatings if she could have anticipated them. As she said in her narrative, "When I got beaten, I never knew it long enough beforehand to pray; and I always thought if I only had *had* time to pray to God for help, I should have escaped the beating."[2]

Isabella prayed that her father would visit her, and he eventually did. Before he departed, she quietly told him how cruelly she was being treated and begged him to rescue her. Not long afterward, a man named Martinus Schryver, who was Dutch like her first two owners, purchased Isabella for $105. Perhaps her father had pleaded with him to do so. Isabella had no doubt that her prayers had been answered.

Schryver was a fisherman and also owned a tavern. He put Isabella to work carrying fish, hoeing corn, and gathering roots and herbs from the woods to make beer. He also sent her to a local shop to buy molasses. He did not beat her, and after a time she began to feel safe. But a year and a half after she went to work for Schryver, he sold her to a man named Dumont. In the Dumont household, Isabella again suffered great cruelty. Mrs. Dumont beat her unmercifully. Still, the Dumonts were more humane than the owners of Robert, a slave with whom she fell in love. An English family named Catlin owned Robert and wanted him to marry one of their female slaves so that the children would be their property. When Robert persisted in visiting Isabella, the Catlins beat him severely and forced him to abandon her. Several months after Robert disappeared from her life, Isabella gave birth to his daughter, whom she named Diana.

Later, when Isabella was seventeen, Mr. Dumont married her to another one of his slaves: Thomas, who was much older than she. Isabella had four children by Thomas. One died in infancy. The others were Peter, Elizabeth, and Sophia. Sophia was born in 1826, one year before the State of New York was due to end slavery. Dumont had promised Isabella that if she worked hard, he would free her that year. Although Isabella worked as hard as she possibly could, he did not keep his promise. After she injured her hand, Dumont said she had failed to be productive.

Isabella was furious and was determined to take her own freedom. As an expression of good faith, she spun 100 pounds of wool into yarn, and then one night just before dawn, she picked up her infant daughter and took refuge with a couple on a nearby farm. When Dumont found her there, the couple, Isaac and Maria Van Wagenen, offered to pay him for the remaining months before the end of slavery took effect.

Once she had settled at the Van Wagenen farm, Isabella set about reclaiming her young son Peter. Dumont had rented him out to another man, who had illegally sold the five-year-old to a slaveholder in Alabama. With the help of Quaker abolitionists, Isabella made an official complaint in court. After months of legal proceedings, Peter was returned to her.

While she was living with the Van Wagenens, Isabella had a life-changing experience when she felt the spirit of God come to her. She began to attend the local Methodist church, where she was drawn to the teachings that God is within everyone. She wanted to know God's word herself, not filtered through the minds of others, and she was frustrated that she was unable to read the Bible. At first, Isabella asked adults to read to her. But she found that they grew impatient with her requests to read the same passage several times. They also tried to explain what they were reading. She didn't want that. She wanted to listen to the words and figure out for herself what God meant. She found that children were much more accommodating and were usually willing to read a passage over and over again without question.

Once Isabella decided that she understood God's truth, she became an inspirational preacher. A white traveling Methodist teacher named Miss Gear persuaded Isabella to accompany her on her travels, so Isabella left her home county in 1829, when she was about thirty-two years old. Not long afterward, she met and was inspired by a religious reformer named Elijah Pierson. He taught that believers should obey the laws of the Old Testament. He held services in his house, which was sometimes called the Kingdom, and attracted a small group of followers.

Isabella moved into the Pierson home as a housekeeper, but she was treated by Pierson as an equal in spiritual matters. After a man named Robert Matthias arrived and challenged Pierson for leadership of the group, the Kingdom began to fall apart. Pierson died in 1834 under mysterious circumstances, and Matthias and Isabella were accused of poisoning him. They were later found innocent of the charges.

Isabella then accompanied Matthias to New York City, where he had influential friends. She kept house for one of them, a wealthy merchant. She joined the John Street Methodist Church for a time, but she was not comfortable being segregated with the other black parishioners from the white congregants. She withdrew and joined Zion's Church, an all-black congregation on Church Street.

In New York, Isabella was reunited with two of her sisters and a brother. She had seen her sister Sophia from time to time, and when Sophia came to New York, she told Isabella that their brother Michael was also living in the city. Further, Isabella was astonished to learn that a fellow parishioner at Zion's Church was another one of her sisters, Nancy.

On June 1, 1843, Isabella announced that God had called her to travel east to bring His message. She changed her name to Sojourner Truth, packed a few belongings in a pillowcase, and set forth. She traveled to Brooklyn, Long Island, and various cities in Connecticut, lecturing and learning the true meaning of God. She had a mission that gave her strength and a deep faith that inspired others to share it.

Eventually, Sojourner Truth found her way to Northampton, Massachusetts, a major industrial center. In 1844, she joined the Northampton Association of Education and Industry. This group of about two hundred people had formed a "utopian community." They believed that the best way to live was together in a cooperative community where everyone worked for the good of the group. They farmed, raised livestock, and operated a gristmill, a sawmill, and a silk factory. The group supported abolition and women's rights. While she was there, Truth met the well-known abolitionists William Lloyd Garrison, who was white; Frederick Douglass, who had escaped slavery; and David Ruggles, a freeborn black man who had founded the first black bookstore in New York City.

Two years after Sojourner Truth joined the community, it went into debt and was forced to sell its land and disband. One of the group's founders, George Benson, had a home and a cotton mill, and Sojourner went to live with him. Meanwhile, she dictated her memoirs to Olive Gilbert, another member of the association. *The Narrative of Sojourner Truth: A Northern Slave* was published privately by William Lloyd Garrison in 1850. It proved very popular, leading to many invitations for Truth to speak at antislavery meetings. With the money she earned, she was able to buy her own home in Northampton.

In 1854, Sojourner was invited to speak at the Ohio Women's Convention in Akron. She gave her most famous speech, addressing the prevailing attitudes toward women—that they were fragile and childlike and in no way equal to men. Sojourner, nearly six feet tall, hardened by work and difficult times, disagreed:

That man over there says that women need to be helped into carriages, and lifted over ditches, and to have the best place everywhere. Nobody ever helps me into carriages, or over mud puddles, or gives me any best place, and ain't I a woman? . . . I have plowed, and planted, and gathered into barns, and no man could head me—and ain't I a woman? I could work as much and eat as much as a man (when I could get it), and bear the lash as well—and ain't I a woman?[3]

Some years later, accused of being a man posing as a woman, Sojourner opened her blouse and bared her breasts. At the time, still seeking a sense of community, she had sold her home in Northampton and was living with a spiritualist group, an offshoot of the Quakers called the Progressive Friends, in Harmonia, Michigan. Like the Northampton group, they believed in abolition and women's rights.

After the Civil War began in 1861, Truth worked for the Union cause. She helped enlist black troops—her own grandson served in the famous all-black regiment, the 54th Massachusetts. She worked as a nurse to freed slaves in a refugee camp off the coast of Virginia and later with the National Freedmen's Relief Association in Washington, D.C. While in the nation's capital, she met President Abraham Lincoln.

Sojourner Truth never ceased her quest to know God and God's truth, but after the Civil War began, she devoted much of her energy to campaigning for her own people. After seeing the desperate conditions of the refugees with whom she worked, she became convinced that they should have their own land and a chance to start new lives. She spent years urging the federal government to make land grants to freed people in the new western territories that were being settled and was delighted to see that many black people were settling in Kansas and creating all-black towns. She spent a year in the Kansas territory, speaking at churches and urging help for newly arrived black settlers.

Sojourner Truth died in 1883 at the age of eighty-six and was buried in a cemetery in Battle Creek, Michigan, where she had moved after leaving Harmonia. By the time she died, her memoirs had been reprinted twice, and she was quite famous as a seeker of many kinds of truth.

NAT
TURNER

(1800–1831)

✦

During the time of slavery, no independent black churches formed in the South. White southerners were far too concerned with the possibility of revolt to allow unguarded gatherings of slaves. The number of free black people in the South was comparatively small, and some southern states had laws against free black people living within their borders. The belief was that they were a bad influence on slaves. Nevertheless, southern enslaved people managed to practice their own religion in secret. They found ways to gather for prayer meetings in the woods at night. Sometimes, just as their owners feared, they used these secret meetings to plan revolts.

Nat Turner was born a slave in Southampton County, Virginia, and was owned by Benjamin Turner. When he was only three or four years old, Nat told his playmates about an event he had witnessed. His mother overheard him and assured him he could not possibly have remembered the event, because it had happened before he was born. Young Nat stuck to his story, and the adults around him began to whisper that he was an extraordinary child with uncommon powers of seeing. As Nat recalled years later, he heard the adults say, "I surely would be a prophet, as the Lord had shewn me things that had happened before my birth. And my father and mother strengthened me in this my first impression, saying in my presence, I was intended for some great purpose."[1] That sense was reinforced when Nat suddenly began to read. Years later, he related that he could not remember how he had learned the alphabet, only that the first time a picture book was shown to him to stop him from crying, he immediately began to spell out the names of the objects depicted. He was a source of wonderment to everyone around him—and a source of great concern to his owner, Benjamin Turner.

Most slaveholders did not want their slaves to learn to read. In fact, there were laws in some areas of the South that barred the teaching of slaves. The reason was that education made slaves restless—reading would expose them to the concept of freedom, as they would understand that there was a big world outside. Slave owners wanted slaves who were just smart enough to do the work that was assigned to them.

Aware that he was considered dangerous because of his intelligence, young Nat Turner kept his thoughts to himself. But he was curious about the world around him. Allowed to attend church, he was struck by the passage in the Bible, "Seek ye the kingdom of Heaven and all things shall be added unto you." He wondered what it meant and often prayed to God to reveal its meaning to him. One day, he was plowing in a field and was overcome by a voice—he decided it was the voice of the same spirit that had spoken to the prophets in the Bible. The voice said to him, "Seek ye the kingdom of Heaven and all things shall be added unto you."[2] For the next two years, Nat prayed every chance he got, anxious to learn what the voice had meant. He studied nature and believed he saw signs. He was certain that his actions were being directed by a higher power.

He started preaching when he was about twenty-five years old, but because he was a slave, he could only preach to his fellow slaves, who looked to him as their leader.

Nat Turner knew from reading the Bible that slavery was wrong. At times, he found ways to rebel. One night, he left the plantation without a pass. Caught by two patrollers, he was severely flogged. He persuaded two young slaves on a neighboring plantation to help him get back at the patrollers. On his instructions, they went out one night and strung a rope across the road that the patrollers usually traveled. Then Turner waited for them to appear. When they did, he started off at a run, avoiding the rope, which caught the two patrollers by surprise and flung them from their horses.

Another time, when Turner's owner hired him out to an especially cruel master, Turner ran away. He was clever and knew the woods, managing to elude capture for a month. But he heard a voice one night that said, "Return to your earthly master, for he who knoweth his Master's will, and doeth it not, shall be beaten with many stripes."[3] So, Nat Turner did as he was bidden. His fellow slaves could not understand why he had returned, for they were certain he was smart enough to have been able to travel north to Canada.

As a child, Nat had been good-natured. But the cruelties of slavery brought about a change in his disposition. As an adult, he developed an intense hatred of all whites. The last of his three owners, Joseph Travis, was a kind man who noted Nat's intelligence and gave him considerable responsibility and freedom. Nat enjoyed the liberties he was given, but Travis's kindness came too late to be appreciated.

Nat spoke of having visions and hearing voices that called him to arms. In 1825, a solar eclipse and an unusual disturbance of the atmosphere occurred, and Turner took them as a sign that he was meant to lead his fellow slaves to freedom. In his vision, Turner saw "white spirits and black spirits engaged in battle, and the sun was darkened, the thunder rolled in the heavens, and blood flowed in streams; and I heard a voice saying, 'Such is your luck; such are you called on to see; and let it come, rough or smooth, you must surely bear it.'"[4]

In 1828, he had another vision. In this one, the spirit appeared and said, "The serpent is loosened, and Christ has laid down the yoke he has borne for the sins of men, and you must take it up, and fight against the serpent, for the time is fast approaching when the first shall be last, and the last shall be first."[5] Turner was struck by the words "The first shall be last, and the last shall be first." He was certain he'd been given a message that it was time to overthrow the whites. Finally, in February 1831, he had yet another vision. A voice told him to arise and prepare himself to slay his enemies with their own weapons.

Nat took his time. Slowly, he confided his intentions to a few of the other slaves, who agreed to assist him in carrying out a plan to kill the Travis family and as many other slave-owning families as they could. They spread the word to slaves they trusted on nearby farms and met secretly in the woods to plot their mission. Late one night in August 1831, all the men met in the woods and prepared a feast, which they cooked over an open fire. They then set off for the Travis home and killed the entire family. They proceeded to neighboring farms, killing the inhabitants, destroying property, and taking money and ammunition. With each assault, they picked up more men. By the time someone managed to raise a general alarm about the rebellion, there were about fifty or sixty men in the Turner band, most of them slaves, although about five were free blacks. All were on horseback and armed with guns, axes, swords, and clubs.

A party of white men set off to find the marauding slaves, and the two groups battled. Several of the Turner men were wounded, and Nat led the others in retreat. They attempted to spend the night on an abandoned farm but were routed by another party of armed whites. Turner found himself alone, his men dead, wounded, or in retreat. He returned to the Travis farm, grabbed as much food as he could, and hid himself under a pile of fence rails in the fields. He remained in hiding for six weeks, leaving his secret place only at night to get water. Two slaves out hunting happened to pass by, and their dog barked. Turner pleaded with the two men not to give him away, but after they left, he decided he could not trust them. He managed to elude capture for another two weeks, but he was finally cornered. Rather than be shot then and there, he gave himself up. The date was October 30, 1831.

Placed in chains and taken to the county jail in Jerusalem, Virginia, Turner knew he faced certain execution. He calmly awaited his trial. Meanwhile, he spoke at some length over the course of several days to his court-appointed attorney, Thomas R. Gray, who had gotten permission from the authorities to interview him. Gray wrote,

> The calm, deliberate composure with which he spoke of his late deeds and intentions, the expression of his fiend-like face when excited by enthusiasm, still bearing the stains of the blood of helpless innocence about him; clothed with rags and covered with chains; yet daring to raise his manacled hands to heaven, with a spirit soaring above the attributes of man; I looked on him and my blood curdled in my veins.[6]

The trial of Nat Turner convened in November 1831. He pleaded not guilty, saying to his counsel that he didn't feel guilty. The account he had given to Thomas Gray was read in court. The defense gave no evidence on his behalf. When asked if he had anything to say as to why he should not be sentenced to death, he said he did not.

According to the black writer William Wells Brown, in a book published in 1863 titled *The Black Man, His Antecedents, His Genius, and His Achievements*, Nat Turner promised that at his death the sun would refuse to shine and the heavens would be disturbed. On the day he was hanged, there was a great storm. People were afraid of him even though he was in chains. Neither the sheriff nor anyone around would do the deed. A poor drunken white man was finally persuaded to be the executioner.

Altogether, fifty-five whites and seventy-three blacks lost their lives in the rebellion. Fifty-three more black people were arrested, including one woman. Several were boys and were sold away, as were some of the men. Twenty-one were convicted. Others were sent on for further trial. A few were discharged or acquitted.

For some years afterward, slaves across the South believed that another rebellion would occur and Nat Turner would reappear to take command. In death, he became an almost mythical figure. "Every eye," wrote William Wells Brown in 1863, while the Civil War was raging, "is now turned towards the south, looking for another Nat Turner."[7]

"Am I not a Woman and a Sister?"

MARIA
STEWART

(1803–1897)

◆

Born free in Hartford, Connecticut, Maria Miller was orphaned at the age of five. As was common in the early 1800s, she was bound out to a local clergyman; that is, she worked as an unpaid servant in exchange for a roof over her head. She was taught Christian values but not otherwise educated, and when she left the clergyman's family at age sixteen, she was determined to get an education.

Maria worked as a domestic servant. On her one day off, she attended Sabbath schools, where she was taught the Bible and enough skills to read and write. When she was in her twenties, she moved to Boston.

The busy port city of Boston had an active abolitionist movement and a strong black middle class. In 1826, Maria Miller married James W.

Stewart, a successful merchant twenty years her senior and a veteran of the War of 1812 who worked as a shipping agent. Stewart believed deeply in abolition and was one of the founders in 1828 of the Massachusetts General Colored Association.

Maria's husband died in 1829, leaving her a widow at the age of twenty-six. By law, she should have inherited her husband's estate, but she was cheated out of her inheritance by white businessmen. Maria turned to religion for solace and soon afterward had a religious awakening. She believed that God had called her to be a warrior for her people, to speak out on behalf of abolition and women's rights. But she did not know how to accomplish her mission. Women weren't even supposed to have political opinions, and they certainly were not supposed to speak or write about politics. Nevertheless, Maria began to write about her feelings concerning liberty.

Those who believed that women should have more rights found sympathy from abolitionists. The leaders of the movement, including Frederick Douglass, born a slave, and William Lloyd Garrison, a prosperous white man, took a broad view of human rights. They believed every human being, including women and slaves, should enjoy the right to life, liberty, and the pursuit of happiness. In 1831, Garrison called on black women to join the abolitionist cause. Seeing her opportunity, Maria Stewart sent her political writings to him. He in turn published them in his abolitionist newspaper, *The Liberator*.

Garrison encouraged Stewart to speak at abolitionist meetings, and she became the first American-born woman of any race to lecture in public on political issues. Because she had been inspired by God to be a warrior for her people, her approach was to preach. She declared that she was an instrument of God, who had called upon her to urge her people to win their own freedom and civil rights. She did not confine herself to antislavery speeches. She asked her people to make the education of their children their mission and to establish strong economic and religious institutions so that the black community did not have to rely on whites.

Maria Stewart also spoke out on women's issues. Particularly memorable was her lecture at the African Masonic Lodge in 1833 criticizing black men for not doing enough for their families and communities. She caused a stir and was criticized for overstepping the bounds of propriety. She left Boston that same year, explaining, "For I find it is no use for me, as an individual, to try to make myself useful among my color in this city."[1]

From then on, Maria Stewart moved about frequently. She settled in New York City for a time, working as a schoolteacher and becoming active in antislavery and women's rights groups. She then moved to Baltimore and eventually to Washington, D.C. In the nation's capital, she finally felt as if she had found a home. She taught in the public schools and opened a Sabbath school for black children near the all-black Howard University. By this time, the Civil War had ended slavery, so she devoted her energies to education.

In 1878, at the age of seventy-five, Maria became eligible for a federal pension as the widow of a veteran of the War of 1812. Her friend William Lloyd Garrison helped her apply for the pension. She used some of the money to publish a collection of her speeches and writings as *Meditations from the Pen of Mrs. Maria W. Stewart*. She died in Washington, D.C., in 1897.

John Jasper

JOHN
JASPER
(1812–1901)

✦

John Jasper was born a slave in Virginia. His parents, Philip and Tina, had twenty-four children, of which John was the youngest. It is possible that he was the product of a difficult birth, for his head was strangely shaped. Years later, his biographer described it this way: "the forehead commencing at the eye-brows and running at an angle of forty-five degrees to the top of the head, where it swells out, while on the rear is a precipice."[1]

Philip Jasper died two months before John was born, but John was raised on stories of his father's deep faith and his skill as a preacher. The Jasper family was owned by a wealthy man named Peachy, who held a number of estates and was in the habit of constantly transferring his slaves from one estate to another. Tina Jasper and her family were sent to a Peachy estate in Williamsburg, where she was assigned to house duties. Most of her children worked in the fields. John started out as a cart boy, helping the ox-cart driver manage the oxen; but he was so smart that he was soon transferred to the house, where he waitered and worked in the garden.

In 1825, when John was about thirteen, Mr. Peachy died. John was hired out to a succession of men in Richmond and Chesterfield counties. Nine or ten years later, Mrs. Peachy died, and the Peachy estate was divided among the Peachy children. John's new owner was John Blair Peachy, who owned farms in Louisiana and planned to take his slaves there. He died before he could do so, however. Once again, John was hired out to various farmers.

Around 1829, while working in Williamsburg, Virginia, John Jasper fell in love with and married a young enslaved woman named Elvy Weaden. Called back to Richmond by his owner, he was not allowed to return to his bride. His owner was afraid that Jasper would do as so many Richmond slaves were doing: escape into the free states. After a while, his wife wrote to tell him that if he could not visit her, she would consider herself free to marry again. He got word back to her that she should do so because it was impossible for him to return to Williamsburg.

Elvy married someone else. In 1844, John also remarried. His second wife, Candus Jordan, bore nine children.

In 1839, when he was twenty-seven years old, John Jasper felt called by God. As he later described the event, he was at work in Samuel Hardgrove's tobacco factory on the morning of July 3—the day before his birthday—when a voice spoke to him. He knew it was the voice of God, calling him to preach God's work. It was the last thing he had expected. He was not an especially religious man and didn't even know the Old Testament from the New Testament. He had never learned to read. He didn't understand how God expected him to preach, and he wondered if the Devil, disguised as God, was playing a trick on him. Years later, Jasper said, "If the Devil spoke to me, he was a bigger fool than I thought he was."[2]

Jasper became convinced that God had called him, so he determined to learn the Bible so that he could do what God had bidden.

While he was teaching himself to read and write, Jasper joined a local black Baptist congregation. The Baptist Church in America goes back to Roger Williams, who established the very first Baptist church in North America when he was exiled from Massachusetts to Rhode Island in 1639. The Baptist Church emphasized a personal relationship with God to which John Jasper responded, and he began attending meetings in the homes of various slave owners. He also began to profess his belief.

In the Baptist Church, you could become a preacher simply by experiencing the call to God. How successful you were depended on your ability to interest your listeners. Jasper was soon well known for his preaching ability.

Jasper was physically imposing—nearly six feet in height, with a high forehead, high cheekbones, a prominent nose, and short, bushy whiskers. His eyes showed a keen intelligence, and his bearing overall suggested a great sense that he had found his mission on earth.

Over time, the Reverend John Jasper became very popular. He received many invitations to preach outside Richmond—primarily at slave funerals. These funerals were usually all-day affairs attended by people from far and wide. Jasper made a deal with his owner that he would pay him out of his preaching salary for the days he missed working at the factory.

After the Civil War broke out, Jasper preached at the Confederate hospitals in Richmond, the capital of the Confederacy. He and his second wife, Candus Jordan, had never gotten along. According to his biographer, Edwin Archer, "After long years of trouble and dissatisfaction Mr. Jasper finally obtained a divorce from her upon good and just grounds."[3] When Union troops threatened Richmond, he moved north, leaving his job at the tobacco factory and relocating to Rolling Mills. He worked at the mills and preached to the mill hands. In September 1863, he married a third time. Mary Anne Cole was a widow with a daughter named Mary Elizabeth, who was about ten at the time of the marriage. The little girl took the last name of Jasper and was raised as his own. He also stayed in touch with his children by Candus Jordan, who were in the Richmond area.

President Abraham Lincoln had issued the Emancipation Proclamation in January 1863. It declared that all slaves in the Confederate states were free, so in theory John Jasper was a free man at that time. But naturally, Confederate slave owners paid no attention to the Union president's laws. Only with the fall of Richmond, the Confederate capital, to Union forces on April 3, 1865, did the war end, and with it, slavery. At the age of fifty-three, the Reverend John Jasper was legally free. He had a total of seventy-three cents and was in debt for his rent.

Following the end of the war and slavery, life in the former Confederate states was greatly disrupted. The major cities were occupied by Union troops, which established temporary occupation governments while the vanquished states wrote new constitutions. Former slaves suddenly were without the protection of their former masters. The entire economy of the South had to be reorganized. The city of Richmond to which the Reverend John Jasper returned was in shambles—its buildings destroyed, its businesses closed, its population scattered. He worked on the streets, cleaning bricks, and he discovered that the usual places for church meetings were gone. Meetings had taken place in the homes of slave owners. Now that there were no slave owners, there were no meeting places.

The Reverend John Jasper did not need a church in which to preach the word of God. He preached wherever he was to whoever would listen. He sought and received authorization from the Freedmen's Bureau to legalize slave marriages. He also helped newly freed black people organize their own churches in Petersburg, Weldon, and Gaston, Virginia. In fact, he was involved in the organization of most of the black Baptist churches in the Richmond area, and no institution grew more quickly among the newly freed black people of the South than the church. By 1884, there were eleven Baptist churches with a total of more than eleven thousand parishioners.

But Jasper wanted to organize his own church, and he did so in September 1867—on Brown's Island just across the James River from

Richmond—in a little wooden structure that had been used as a govern-ment stable. It was called the Sixth Mount Zion Church—not because there were five other Mount Zion churches in the area but because the founders liked the name. It was more commonly known as Jasper's Church. The congregation increased quickly. When they had outgrown the little shack, they moved across the river to a carpenter's shop in Richmond.

Eventually, they raised the money to buy a small brick church build-ing in the northwestern part of the city that was so heavily populated by black people that it was called Africa. The advantage of being in a black ward was that black people, now free and under Union occupa-tion, had political control. Although the Reverend John Jasper could have used his influence to enter politics, he did not. He believed he had been chosen by God to bring His word to the people, and he did not stray from that mission.

Like his parishioners, he was uneducated and ungrammatical in his speech. Also like his parishioners, he brought high emotion to his faith. For centuries, the practice of religion had been the only part of life in which slaves could let themselves go and give full vent to their feelings. The Reverend Jasper embodied that religious emotionalism. His biogra-pher described his preaching style:

> He circled around the pulpit with his ankle in his hand; and laughed and sang and shouted and acted about a dozen charac-ters within the space of three minutes. Meanwhile, in spite of these things, he was pouring out a gospel sermon, red hot, full of love, full of invective, full of tenderness, full of bitterness, full of tears, full of every passion that ever flamed in the human breast. . . . He was the preacher; likewise the church and the choir and the deacons and the congregation.[4]

Jasper became the most famous black preacher in the Richmond area—and, according to his biographer, had a greater reputation in Europe than any other southern man since the end of the Civil War. He owed his notoriety to a sermon entitled "Sun Do Move."

For centuries, scientists and philosophers had accepted the idea that the earth revolves around the sun and that it is not the sun but the earth that moves. But the Reverend John Jasper believed in the literal word of the Bible, and to his mind the Bible made it clear that the sun does move. He based a powerful sermon on this, and it became his most famous.

Naturally, that sermon inspired great controversy. Some people called him illiterate. Others called him a liar. His strongest critics were young, educated black preachers who had attended seminary schools in the North, then relocated to the Richmond area after Federal troops occupied the vanquished South. They looked down on him with his high-emotion preaching and his ungrammatical way of speaking. They considered him an embarrassment. They thought they could quiet him. But Jasper would not be cowed. In fact, he questioned the faith of the educated, well-spoken black preachers.

Ebenezer Baptist Church called a conference to discuss the issue and summoned Jasper to attend. He refused, saying that the church had no right to interfere. Letters and articles appeared in local papers and in periodicals as far away as Europe. Jasper undertook speaking tours to northern cities, all based on that one sermon. He was so steadfast in his conviction that eventually even those who criticized him came to respect his utter belief in the literal interpretation of the Bible.

The Reverend John Jasper died on March 30, 1901. His last words were "I have finished my work and am down at the river waiting for further orders."[5] The *Richmond Dispatch* called him a "Richmond Institution," and indeed he was the last of the old-style, pre–Civil War preachers. His body was buried in the old Mechanics Cemetery. When the city condemned that cemetery in the course of growth, his remains were carried, with appropriate ceremony, to Richmond's Woodlawn Cemetery, and his grave was marked with a large granite shaft. The Sixth Mount Zion Baptist Church exists today, with a John Jasper Memorial Room dedicated to its most famous preacher.

ALEXANDER
CRUMMELL

(1819–1898)

and

HENRY HIGHLAND
GARNETT

(1815–1882)

◆

Born just seven years after John Jasper, Alexander Crummell lived in conditions and had experiences that were a world away from Jasper's. Crummell was born free in New York City. The story goes that as a young man, Alexander's father, Boston Crummell, announced to his owner that he would no longer be a slave, and he left his owner's household. Boston Crummell worked for the abolition of slavery. Alexander grew up in a household where men like John B. Russworm, the first black doctor, Samuel Cornish, a minister and abolitionist, and other prominent blacks were frequent visitors. Unlike most African Americans at the time, the Crummell family belonged to the Episcopal Church.

Alexander Crummell attended the city's First African Free School. His classmates included Ira Aldridge, who would go on to become a noted actor, and Henry Highland Garnett, who had been born a slave in the South but moved to the North with his family. White abolitionists helped Crummell and Garnett get further education, and both men enrolled in Noyes Academy in Canaan, New Hampshire, which had been established by abolitionists for the education of black youth. After local people attacked the school and dragged the building down with a team of oxen, the two young men enrolled at the Oneida Institute in Whitesboro, New York. The local population there accepted the school, and both Garnett and Crummell completed their college education.

Crummell pursued his dream to be a priest in the Episcopal Church. He moved to Boston, where he was ordained in the Massachusetts Diocese at the age of twenty-five. But he encountered severe racism in the church. Denied admission to church meetings, he left Boston, and again aided by abolitionist friends, Crummell traveled to England in 1847 for further schooling. He earned his degree from Queens College, Cambridge, in 1853. Meanwhile, Henry Highland Garnett had become a minister in New York City.

The two young men had more in common than being men of the church. Both had concluded that there was no place for them or their people in American society.

In 1787, Great Britain had helped four hundred freed slaves from its own country, Nova Scotia, and the United States to settle in Sierra Leone on the west coast of Africa, where the British established Freetown, calling it the Province of Freedom. They hoped it would serve not only as a homeland for freed slaves but also as an outpost for British trade interests in Africa. Inspired by the British action, Paul Cuffe, a wealthy black American ship owner in Connecticut, transported a group of thirty-eight African Americans to Sierra Leone in 1815 and provided a cargo of supplies to get them started in their new home. Cuffe was unable to pursue his dream further, however, for his health failed and he died two years later.

In 1816, white Americans formed the American Colonization Society, whose purpose was similar to that of the British colonizers. The organization was supported by three groups with very different aims. One group was mostly white Quakers who wanted to free African slaves and their descendants and provide them with the opportunity to return to Africa. The second group was slave owners who feared that the growing number of free people of color was a danger to their way of life and wanted them gone from America. The third group was black Americans who despaired of ever being able to live free in the United States. The American Colonization Society established the colony of Liberia, next to Sierra Leone on the west coast of Africa, as a new home for freed American blacks.

Alexander Crummell moved to Freetown in Sierra Leone in 1853 and spent nearly twenty years working to make the two settlements of free blacks on the west coast of Africa successful.

Crummell believed that African Americans were ideal missionaries to Africa. He wrote that they were, by heritage, well suited to the tropical climate, adding that they also knew the "sorrow, pain, and deepest anguish" of slavery and thus were uniquely suited to work on a continent that had been virtually enslaved by European colonizers. He was sure that, "The hand of God is on the black man, in all the lands of his distant sojourn, for the good of Africa. This continent is to be reclaimed for Christ. The faith of Jesus is to supersede all the abounding desolations of heathenism."[1]

For most of the years Crummell spent doing missionary work in West Africa, he lived in Liberia and served as professor of mental and moral science at the College of Liberia. He wrote and published a book, *Future of Africa*, in 1862. He believed firmly in the vision of a black Christian republic of freed slaves. But eventually he became

African Religions

Many cultures existed on the huge continent of Africa, and each society had its own religious system. Many of these systems were based on geography and the different societies' views of the place of humans in nature. Hunting peoples focused on the power of the forest and the spirits of animals, while herding peoples had strong beliefs in sky gods. All African societies recognized the power of ancestors and of their ties to others in the group. Some societies were guided by special priests; in other societies the ruler was a sacred figure. Some societies worshipped one god; others, many gods.

By the time European nations established the slave trade on the west coast of Africa, Islam had made major inroads on the continent. By the seventh century A.D., North Africans from the Arabian Peninsula had sailed down the eastern coast of the continent and crossed the vast Sahara Desert to trade with the African peoples. After the religion of Islam was founded by Muhammad (A.D. 570 to 632), Arabs went southward in ever-increasing numbers to spread the faith.

disillusioned with the political life in the two grand experiments in African settlement.

The free and freed African Americans who arrived on the west coast of Africa to make a new life had little in common with each other and even less with the native Africans. The native peoples resisted both the intrusion of the newcomers and attempts by the newcomers to convert them to Christianity. During the nineteenth century, the native peoples mounted several unsuccessful revolts against British rule and the former slaves from the British Empire. Eventually, the British divided Sierra Leone into two distinct parts: Freetown, a colony dominated by the newcomers, and the rest of Sierra Leone, in which the native peoples held sway. Similar unrest dominated the political life of Liberia.

His health failing, Crummell left Africa in 1872 and returned to the United States, settling in Washington, D.C. He had a vision of the black church as a place of worship and social service, and he established Saint

Luke's Church in 1880 to serve as a model for the role he felt the church should play in black life. He organized the black Episcopal clergymen to fight racism in the church and encouraged other black priests and ministers in the city to work together to establish charitable institutions to help the city's black population.

Crummell also emphasized the need for education as a way to overcome racism and poverty. He believed in the power of education for the betterment of both Africans and African Americans. He helped to establish the American Negro Academy, an organization of educated African Americans, and wrote two more books, *Greatness of Christ* (1882) and *Africa and America* (1892), and many essays.

Crummell maintained a strong interest in African missions. A man very much of his time, he accepted the image of Africa as a dark continent without a civilization and never sought to appreciate African culture and religion. Raised and educated in Western traditions, including Christianity, he believed that Africa was uncivilized and that the best way for Africans to improve their lives was to adopt Western values and traditions. He wrote, "Civilization . . . never springs up, spontaneously, in any new land. It must be transplanted."[2]

Alexander Crummell died in Washington, D.C., in 1898.

When Alexander Crummell was in Sierra Leone in 1853, Henry Highland Garnett was on an extended trip to Great Britain, sent there by the Free Labor Movement, an antislavery organization, to speak for the abolition of slavery in the United States. After poor health forced him to return home, he became pastor of Shiloh Church on Prince Street in New York City.

Garnett had become convinced that black people could never be equal in the United States and he worked hard for emigration to Africa. Like his friend Alexander Crummell, he believed that American black people could serve humanity by bringing Christian civilization to Africa. In 1859, he founded the African Civilization Society and made plans to visit Africa, but the outbreak of the Civil War in 1863 forced him to put those plans on hold.

Garnett turned his attention to recruiting black men to fight for the Union. In 1864, he moved to Washington, D.C., and served as pastor of Fifteenth Street Presbyterian Church. Four years later, he accepted the position of president of Avery College in Pittsburgh, Pennsylvania, and served there until 1870, then returned to Shiloh Church in New York City. During the next decade, in spite of chronic health problems, he campaigned for the post of U.S. Minister to Liberia and finally received that appointment in 1881. He arrived in Monrovia, the capital of Liberia, in December and died less than two months later, on February 12, 1882.

PART THREE

LEADERS OF THE RECONSTRUCTION ERA AND THE EARLY TWENTIETH CENTURY

H E N R Y M C N E A L

TURNER

(1833–1915)

◆

Henry McNeal Turner was born on a plantation in South Carolina, the first child of Howard and Sarah Turner, but he was not born into slavery. His father's mother had been German and white. His mother's father had been the son of an African king, who was brought to South Carolina when it was still a British colony. Young Henry was light-complexioned, with deep-set eyes and chubby cheeks, a dreamer in circumstances that defied dreaming.

The Turners were poor, and as soon as Henry was old enough to work, he labored in the cotton fields. Later, he was apprenticed to a blacksmith. When he was very young, he had a dream that set him on his life's mission. He dreamed that he was standing on a mountain, and below him were millions of people of all kinds looking to him for instruction. When he woke up, he decided that it was his call to be a leader of his people.

Young Henry Turner knew that he needed an education to be a leader. That would be difficult in South Carolina, which had laws that prohibited black people from learning to read. An elderly white woman who lived nearby and a white playmate taught him the alphabet. But his playmate's father saw what they were doing and put a stop to it. Henry Turner persevered, getting help from anyone who had the least bit of learning.

One Sunday when he was thirteen, he was in church when he heard the preacher say, "Whatever anyone asks God for in faith would be granted."[1] So, Henry decided to ask God to help him read and write. He prayed and prayed, and soon his mother surprised him by announcing that she had found a white woman to give him lessons every Sunday. Those lessons ended when local whites threatened Henry's tutor with arrest. He continued to pray and study on his own, dreaming nearly every night that an angel appeared to teach him what he needed to know.

When he was fifteen, Turner went to work for an office of white attorneys. He swept the floors, tended the fires, and did other janitorial work. But soon the lawyers discovered that he had an amazing memory and that he was the perfect messenger. No matter how many words or numbers a message contained, or how many legal terms, Henry Turner could repeat it with as much accuracy as if he were reading it on a piece of paper. The younger lawyers in the firm took it upon themselves to defy the law and teach him history, theology, and law. He later said, "I shall always regard my contact with those lawyers, and the assistance given by the young lawyers of the office, as an answer to my prayer."[2]

Turner joined the Methodist Episcopal Church South in 1848, when he was still a teenager. He was given provisional membership in the predominantly white church. Years later, he joked that he must still be on probation because he had never been received into full membership. He continued to study the Bible and was known to memorize fifty psalms before going to sleep at night. In 1853, he was licensed to preach.

In 1856, he married Eliza Ann Peacher of Columbia, South Carolina, the daughter of the wealthiest black man in the city. The couple would have a total of fourteen children.

In 1857, Turner visited New Orleans, Louisiana, and met the Reverend W. R. Revels, M.D., who was not only a minister in the African Methodist Episcopal (AME) Church but also a doctor. Influenced greatly by the Reverend Revels, Turner transferred his church membership to the AME Church. He was licensed as an itinerant preacher in 1858 and assigned to a small parish in Baltimore, Maryland.

In Baltimore, Turner met more educated and cultured people than he had ever known before. He worked hard to deliver sermons that would appeal to them. He was embarrassed when he heard that one of his parishioners complained about his grammar. He spent the next four years studying not just English grammar but also Latin, Greek, Hebrew, and German, as well as theology. He was ordained a deacon in 1860 and an elder in 1862 when he was only thirty years old.

When the Civil War broke out in 1861, many black men yearned to serve in the Union Army, but it was not until 1863 that President Abraham Lincoln gave the order to accept black men. The Reverend Henry M. Turner helped organize the first black regiment of U.S. troops in his own churchyard. He was appointed chaplain to Company B of the First U.S. Colored Troops in the early part of 1863. Turner was the first commissioned black chaplain ever appointed by a U.S. president. He saw thirteen battles and many skirmishes with his company before he was mustered out with his regiment in the fall of 1865. He was then recommissioned U.S. chaplain in the regular army by President Andrew Johnson and assigned to work in the Freedmen's Bureau in Georgia.

Turner did what he could under the Reconstruction government, but he felt he could make a much larger contribution by returning to his religious calling. During Reconstruction, the churches became the freedmen's first social centers, the places where they turned for help in adjusting to their new circumstances. Turner traveled throughout Georgia, Alabama, and Tennessee, preaching, lecturing, and organizing churches and schools. Eventually, he built up a conference, or periodic meeting of church leaders, that was not only the largest in the AME Church but the largest black church group in the world.

After the Reconstruction laws were passed by Congress in 1867, southern black men had the vote (no women, black or white, could vote then, and they would not get the vote until 1920) for a brief, exciting time and were able to hold office. Turner was appointed by the National Republican Executive Committee in Washington, D.C., to organize the black people of Georgia into a state Republican Party. He traveled throughout the state, delivering speeches and writing campaign brochures. He worked for the election of black men whom he considered worthy and was himself elected a member of the Georgia Constitutional Convention in the fall of 1867 and to the Reconstruction state legislature of Georgia in 1868.

The white people of Georgia hated having people of color in such powerful positions. They used intimidation and violence to keep black people from voting. In 1868, the white members of the Georgia legislature voted to expel the African Americans who had been elected. Turner vehemently and eloquently objected. Soon afterward, he received threats on his life from the Ku Klux Klan, a violent white supremacist group.

The U.S. Congress forced the Georgia legislature to readmit the black members in 1870, but Turner was denied reelection in a fraud-filled contest a few months later. For a time, Turner served as postmaster of Macon, Georgia, on the appointment of President Ulysses S. Grant. He later worked as coast inspector of customs, also a presidential appointment. During his time in Georgia, he also served as chancellor of Morris Brown College (now Morris Brown University) in Atlanta for twelve years. Although he accepted government positions, Turner was critical of the U.S. government for failing to live up to the promises of the post–Civil War amendments to the Constitution. He railed against the steady ebbing of African American rights.

In 1876, Turner was elected by the general conference of the AME Church as general manager of the publication department in Philadelphia, Pennsylvania. He wrote or edited all the papers and Sabbath school literature that the church distributed in the United States.

He used his position to publish hymnals and policy books on AME Church practice. He also used it to propound his notions of black Christian faith, which included the idea of a black Christ. Turner wrote:

> We have as much right biblically and otherwise to believe that God is a Negroe [sic] as you buckra ["devils"] or white people have to believe that God is a fine looking, symmetrical and ornamented white man. . . . Every race of people who have attempted to describe their God by words, or by paintings, or by carvings, or any other form or figure, have conveyed the idea that the God who made them and shaped their destinies was symbolized in themselves, and why should not the Negroe believe that he resembles God.[3]

In 1880, in a hard-fought and controversial contest, Turner won election as the twelfth bishop of the AME Church. Five years after that, he became the first AME bishop to ordain a woman, Sarah Ann Hughes, to the office of deacon.

Turner's wife, Eliza, died in 1889. He married three more times, in 1893, 1900, and 1907. During those years, he was active in the back-to-Africa cause. He became a supporter of the West African colony of Liberia, settled by African Americans both freeborn and freed. His first father-in-law was also a champion of Liberia. In fact, Joseph A. Peacher left the United States and settled in Liberia, where he was elected mayor of the town of Careysburg.

Turner made four trips to Africa between 1891 and 1898. He enlisted the support of white businessmen in Alabama to organize the International Migration Society and established his own newspapers to promote his organization and its cause. He managed to attract around five hundred migrants to fill two ships, which sailed to Liberia in 1895 and 1896. Although a number of the migrants returned, complaining about disease, lack of economic opportunity, and political troubles with the native Africans, he did not lose faith.

Turner died in Windsor, Ontario, in 1915 while visiting a settlement of black men and women who had fled to Canada to escape the American fugitive slave laws in the years before the Civil War.

BOYD

(1843–1922)

◆

Richard Henry Boyd was born a slave on the B. A. Gray plantation in Nexubee County, Mississippi. He was one of ten children and was given the name Dick Gray by his owner. (In 1867, he changed his name from Dick Gray to Richard Henry Boyd.) As soon as he was old enough, Boyd was put to work planting and harvesting cotton. He was in his late teens when the Civil War began. The men in the Gray family enlisted in the Confederate Army, and Boyd accompanied them into battle. It was common for slave owners who served in the Confederate Army to be accompanied by one of their slaves as a body servant.

Between August and November 1863, Confederate and Union armies battled in the vicinity of Chattanooga, Tennessee, where the Grays were stationed. In a clever move, Union general William Rosecrans sent forces northwest of the city to divert the attention of the

Confederate forces under General Braxton Bragg, who sent his troops to forestall the Union threat, leaving himself vulnerable to the south. As the two armies battled northwest of the city, another Union force approached through the rugged mountain passes to the south. By the time the Confederates realized what had happened, it was too late. Bragg ordered his troops to withdraw from the Chattanooga area, allowing Union forces to occupy the city without a shot. Many historians believe that this was the beginning of the end for the Confederacy in the Civil War.

The elder Gray and his two older sons were killed near Chattanooga. The youngest son was seriously wounded, and Boyd took him back to the Gray plantation. The plantation, like so many others across the South, had suffered while the owner and his sons were off fighting. Boyd took over the job of running it, even though he remained a slave. Under his management, the plantation produced substantial cotton crops. Boyd also assumed the task of selling the crops, traveling to Mexico to trade cotton.

Boyd did not leave the Gray plantation until the Civil War and slavery ended. He decided to go to Texas, through which he had traveled on his way to Mexico. Many freed people were moving to the western frontier, where land was inexpensive and opportunities were plentiful. Boyd worked for a time as a cowboy and later as a sawmill laborer.

He was a tall man, light-complexioned, with aquiline features. He had some knowledge of reading and writing, and after emancipation he was determined to educate himself. Studying alone and with the help of friends, Boyd later enrolled at Bishop College in Marshall, Texas. He also married Hattie Albertine Moore and started a family.

Boyd became a Baptist minister in 1869. In 1872, he helped to organize other black Baptist ministers in the state as the Negro Baptist Convention of Texas. He started with six churches and steadily built the organization until it represented nearly all the black Baptist congregations in the state.

Boyd was troubled by the lack of books for African American Baptists. He believed that black people should publish their own literature and guide the minds of their own children. He published two pamphlets for use in black Baptist Sunday schools in 1894 and 1895. He thought about starting a black Baptist publishing company. Nashville, Tennessee, was the headquarters of the Southern Baptist Convention, the umbrella organization for all southern Baptist churches. In 1896, he moved his family to Nashville to pursue his mission.

The Boyd family joined Mount Olivet Baptist Church, and Boyd persuaded the pastor of the church, the Reverend C. H. Clark, to help him start his publishing company. The white director of the Southern Baptist Convention's Sunday school press also agreed to help him. Boyd formed the National Baptist Publishing Board. In 1897, with printing plates on loan from the white Baptist Publishing Board, he issued his first publications.

Boyd was a tireless worker for the black Baptist Church and for educational opportunities for black people. He worked for the American Missionary Convention, the American Foreign Mission Convention, and the Education Convention. He either helped to establish or supported Bishop College, Guadalupe College, Boyd's Normal Institute, Central Texas College, Roger Williams University, and the National Baptist Theological and Missionary Training Seminary in Nashville. He was a member of the faculty of the seminary. He wrote more than fourteen books, including *Plantation Melody Songs*, *Theological Kernals*, *An Outline of Negro Baptist History*, and *The Story of the Publishing Board*. All of them were published by his company.

The National Baptist Publishing Board was so successful that some leaders of the Southern Baptist Convention tried to persuade Boyd to incorporate it and make it an official business. Boyd steadfastly refused to do so, but he was not averse to profitable businesses. In fact, he believed that black people should start their own businesses instead of patronizing those of whites. In 1904, he was the founder and first president of the One Cent Savings Bank and Trust Company. Another business he started was the National Baptist Convention Supply Company. He used his knowledge of publishing to start the Nashville Globe Printing Company and a weekly African American newspaper, *Nashville*

Bishop C. M. "Sweet Daddy" Grace (1881–1960)

Also entrepreneurial in his own way was Charles Manuel Grace, one of the most charismatic and colorful of the black "messiahs" of early twentieth-century America. He was born Marcelino Manoel da Graca in the Portuguese Cape Verde Islands in 1881 and came to America with his family in the early 1900s. The family settled in the port city of New Bedford, Massachusetts, but Manoel did not seek work on the docks when he was old enough to get a job. Instead, he worked on a railroad line as a short-order cook, as a salesman, and in a grocery store. He married Jennie J. Combard on February 2, 1909, and divorced her in 1920.

At some point, he Anglicized his name from Manoel Graca to Charles Manuel Grace. He also joined a Pentecostal church. The Pentecostal movement was an outgrowth of Evangelical Christianity, which had arisen in the late nineteenth century. Evangelical Christianity emphasizes a direct personal relationship with God. Pentecostals have similar beliefs and pay special attention to baptism and the biblical account of the Day of Pentecost, when the Holy Spirit descended upon the apostles and other followers of Jesus Christ.

Grace felt the call to preach and became a charismatic who claimed to possess the Holy Spirit, urging his followers to feel the power of the Holy Spirit by expressing their ecstasy and speaking in tongues. He took immediately to Pentecostalism and became a preacher in the church. By 1921, he had established his own church, the United House of Prayer for All People.

Grace's church featured brass "shout bands," and he preached fiery sermons, captivating many poor black people in New Bedford. There were many church offices, and about one-quarter of the members held some sort of position, which guaranteed their loyalty.

Grace also dispensed considerable charity to the poor. Much later, during the Great Depression of the 1930s, when there were House of Prayer churches in many northern cities, hungry and impoverished black people could go to Daddy Grace's soup kitchens and get an entire meal for thirty-five cents.

(continued)

Bishop C. M. "Sweet Daddy" Grace *(continued)*

Daddy Grace was an excellent fund-raiser. He developed and sold a line of products that included Daddy Grace coffee, tea, soaps, and hand creams. He had grand houses and cars and a devoted loyal following. Although after his death in 1960 the church was fined millions of dollars in unpaid taxes, the Church of Prayer remains strong in many cities today. With headquarters in Washington, D.C., it is estimated to have 3.5 million members.

Globe and Independent. His son, Henry Allen Boyd, was his partner in this effort. Boyd even started the National Negro Doll Company, the first in the nation to manufacture ethnic dolls.

Boyd became a leader in Nashville's black community. He used his position to champion the 1905 boycott of the city's streetcar lines by black riders to protest segregation on the streetcars. He died in 1922 at the age of seventy-nine, easily the most entrepreneurial African American religious leader of that time.

VERNON
JOHNS
(1892–1965)

✦

Vernon Johns is widely regarded as the father of the U.S. civil rights movement. He laid the foundation for resistance to white supremacy and segregation on which Martin Luther King Jr. and others would build their movements.

Johns was born in Darlington Heights, Virginia, during the worst era for African Americans since slavery times. Reconstruction had ended and the Jim Crow era had begun—a period during which black people were legally separated from white people in all areas of community life.

Vernon Johns's parents were sharecroppers. Schooling for black children was minimal to nonexistent, so Johns educated himself. He read while he plowed the fields. At night, he squinted to see the words on the page as he read by candlelight. He started with the Bible and was soon able to recite long passages. He was said to have a photographic

Jim Crow Laws

Jim Crow was a minstrel character—a white man named Thomas "Daddy" Rice who took the stage name Jim Crow and became famous for his impersonation of an old black man with a gimpy leg who did a funny jig. Somehow, the term *Jim Crow* came to be applied to

the raft of laws that were passed in the South after Reconstruction ended in 1877. The laws aimed to segregate, or separate, black people from white society. Beginning with laws that established separate railroad cars for black passengers, these laws eventually included local ordinances that prevented blacks and whites from playing checkers together in public or looking out a factory window at the same time.

Black people did not allow segregation to become law without a fight. Beginning in the early 1880s, they challenged those laws in court. The most famous opposition to legal segregation was by Homer Plessy, a black man who brought suit against the Louisiana railroad company that forced him to sit in a Jim Crow car. His case, *Plessy* v. *Ferguson*, went all the way to the U.S. Supreme Court.

Before the Supreme Court, Plessy's attorneys argued that segregation violated the Fourteenth Amendment to the U.S. Constitution, which held that no state could pass any law that denied the privileges of citizenship. On May 18, 1896, a majority of the justices on the court decided that separate accommodations were constitutional as long as they were equal. That "separate but equal" decision allowed the system of legal segregation in the South to continue for more than sixty years.

memory. He read every book he could get his hands on, including religious books written in Greek, Latin, Hebrew, and German.

Johns became a Baptist preacher, but he was not content to remain a self-educated minister. By 1915, he was ready to attend college. He wrote to the dean of Oberlin College in Ohio, listing his self-teaching accomplishments and asking to be admitted as a regular student. He received a letter from Oberlin telling him that he did not have enough credits to enroll.

Johns had a fiery temper and a strong sense of himself. He refused to take no for an answer. He traveled to Oberlin and asked to see the dean. Granted an audience with the deputy dean, he demanded, "I want to know whether you want students with credits or students with brains."[1] Impressed by his determination, the deputy dean took Johns's case to the dean, Edward Increase Bosworth, who tested him in the reading of Greek scripture. After Johns proved he could indeed read Greek scripture, Bosworth admitted him on a trial basis. By the end of the semester, he had won a place as a regular student. He supported himself by preaching part-time.

Oberlin College was an oasis of equality, but it was predominantly white and not free of racism. The top student at Oberlin at the time, Robert M. Hutchins, said it was impossible for a "country Negro" like Johns to get such good grades without cheating. Johns responded by punching Hutchins in the mouth. The two eventually became close friends.

After graduating from Oberlin in 1918, Johns enrolled in the graduate school of theology at the University of Chicago. He had an equally stellar career as a student there. He had many offers from churches, but he did not keep any job long. He refused to bow to racism or hypocrisy, and he did not feel that he fit into conventional church life. He much preferred being a traveling preacher and was on the road for months at a time, doing odd jobs to support himself.

Eventually, however, he decided to settle down. In 1947, Johns accepted the position of pastor of the Dexter Avenue Baptist Church in Montgomery, Alabama. Its congregation was made up of the elite of black Montgomery, which meant that they were allowed to prosper as long as they kept their place and accepted segregation. They had to send their children to inferior schools, drink from water fountains marked "Colored," sit in the back of the city bus, and give up their seats if white riders were standing. They could not register to vote; they could not try on clothing or shoes in white-owned stores; they could not eat in white-owned restaurants.

Tired of being an itinerant preacher, the Reverend Johns tried to accept the way things were in Montgomery. But at length he just couldn't take it. One day, he boarded a city bus and tried to sit in the white section. When the bus driver refused to allow him to do so, Johns demanded his fare back and got it. Another day, Johns entered a white-owned restaurant and ordered a meal. He was told to leave. Angry that he could not enjoy the same rights as white people, he started speaking out against segregation from his pulpit, scolding his congregation for accepting things as they were. His demands made the parishioners uncomfortable. When he threatened to resign if the church leaders didn't start taking a stand, the deacons of the Dexter Avenue Baptist Church accepted his resignation.

In 1952, at the age of sixty, the Reverend Johns went back to being a traveling preacher. He never again held a full-time position as a minister at a church. But he had the pleasure of seeing his successor at the Dexter Avenue Baptist Church, a young man named Martin Luther King Jr., rise to a leadership position in the Montgomery Bus Boycott, which started three years after he left. He watched as the citizens of Montgomery refused to ride the city buses until they could sit anywhere they chose. He watched as King and other southern Baptist ministers led the direct-action civil rights movement that culminated in the passage of the 1964 Civil Rights Act, which outlawed segregation. He died in 1965 knowing that he had laid the groundwork for their accomplishments.

Elijah

MUHAMMAD

(1897–1975)

◆

Elijah Muhammad was born Elijah Poole in Sandersville, Georgia, one of thirteen children. His parents were sharecroppers, or tenant farmers, which meant that they worked hard and never managed to get ahead. The southern sharecropper system was designed to keep black people in virtual slavery. Sharecroppers, or tenant farmers, rented the land they worked and the houses in which they lived from white farmers. They bought farm equipment and feed on credit from white-owned stores. They paid their rent and their store bill with a share of the harvest. Their own "share" usually ended up being nothing. Floods, droughts, and locusts could wipe out a crop, leaving the sharecropper owing his farmer landlord until the next year. Even in a good year, the whites in power conspired to make sure that tenant farmers had little or nothing to show for all their labor.

Segregation was as severe in Georgia as it was in Alabama. Anyone who resisted it could be beaten or killed. Young Elijah Poole was determined not to live the life of a sharecropper. When he was sixteen years old, he left home. He traveled around, working odd jobs to support himself and witnessing more evidence of racism. By 1917, when he was twenty years old, he had reportedly witnessed three lynchings, or killings of black people by white mobs. He hated white people.

Also when he was twenty, Poole married a young woman named Clara. It was his desire to provide for his wife and the children they hoped to have, as well as his hatred of segregation, which led to his moving to Detroit.

World War I had just ended, and even when the United States had remained out of the fighting, its industries had provided military supplies to U.S. allies in Europe. Northern industries were booming, so there were many jobs to be had. Black southerners migrated north in droves, seeking not only jobs but the opportunity to live like human beings. There was plenty of racism in the North, but it was not the crushing segregation of the South. Detroit, Michigan, was already known as the center of the American automobile industry, and Elijah Poole got a job in an auto plant.

In the early 1930s, Poole met a man named W. D. Fard, who had attracted a significant following among black people in the city by preaching that the true religion of African Americans was Islam. This idea was not original to Fard. In 1913, a man named Noble Drew Ali (born Timothy Drew in 1886 in North Carolina) had opened a Moorish Science Temple in Newark, New Jersey, where he preached that black Americans were of Moorish (Moroccan) descent and thus of Muslim heritage. Ali's claim that African Americans were Muslim by heritage had some basis in fact, for many of the Africans brought as slaves to the New World had been followers of Islam.

Noble Drew Ali preached a faith that differed markedly from world Islam, which was founded in the seventh century A.D. by the Arab religious and political figure Mohammed (also spelled Muhammad). Mohammed believed in the same God (*Allah* in Arabic) as Christians and

Jews and preached total surrender to Him (*Islam* means submission). He set down a system of beliefs and practices, including dietary laws, in a book called the *Qur'an*. He did not claim to establish a new religion but to restore the original faith of Abraham, Moses, and Jesus, whom he called prophets like himself. Followers of Ali's temple refused to fight in World War I, incurring the hatred of many of the people of Newark. Fearing attack, Ali relocated his Moorish Science Temple movement to Chicago, where he continued to urge black Americans to reject European labels such as "black" and "colored" and for all Americans to reject hate and embrace love.

Fard elaborated greatly on Ali's version of Islam. Fard's version included a complicated creation myth that featured an evil scientist named Dr. Yakub. He also proclaimed that black Americans were the Lost Found Nation of Islam, the descendants of the Asian Black Nation and of the tribe of Shabazz. Fard said that black Americans must find themselves and that they should start by casting off their slave names and asking him for their "original" names. He attracted many followers, and soon he founded Temple No. 1 of the Nation of Islam in Detroit. As his following grew, he established a security force called the Fruit of Islam and a school called the University of Islam.

Membership in the Nation of Islam (NOI) was a way of life. Temple services and meetings were held several times a week. Men and women followed strict rules governing relationships between them; husbands and wives each had duties to the family. Members were admonished to work hard, save their money, and give a fixed percentage of their income to the Nation. By following the rules of the Nation, many formerly poor, illiterate, and hopeless black people became stable and prosperous. The NOI had great appeal to Elijah Poole's family. Several members joined, giving up their slave names in favor of names bestowed upon them by Fard. Elijah was given the name Karriem.

Disagreements and factionalism threatened the Nation of Islam almost from the start. W. D. Fard's willingness to have his Fruit of Islam take up arms disturbed some members, as did his teaching that his followers were not Americans and owed no loyalty to their country of birth.

In spite of these disagreements, the Nation of Islam grew. Temple No. 2 was established in Chicago and the beginnings of what would become Temple No. 3 in Milwaukee. By 1934, the Nation had an estimated membership of about eight thousand. Karriem, the former Elijah Poole, had become indispensable to Fard, and when it came time for Fard to name a minister of Islam to take over the daily operations of the movement, he chose Karriem, giving him a new name, Elijah Muhammad, to acknowledge his elevated status.

Shortly thereafter, Fard disappeared, leaving Elijah Muhammad with little preparation for leading the Nation of Islam. The NOI was ridden with factionalism, and membership began to decline. Detroit Temple No. 1 was especially in disarray. After threats were made on Muhammad's life, he left the city. He tried to relocate to Chicago, but factionalism forced him to flee. He then moved to Washington, D.C., where he began Temple No. 4; but eventually he made peace with the Chicago factions and made that city his headquarters.

Muhammad continued the teachings of Fard: that black people were the Lost Found Nation, that whites were evil, and that members of the NOI must obey the rules of dress, diet, and decorum. He emphasized that black people must be independent of whites. He bought land, opened businesses, and built schools. He established a newspaper, *Muhammad Speaks*, and founded temples in two additional cities.

The Nation of Islam, whose members were often called Black Muslims by outsiders, was especially successful in attracting converts among prison populations. One of them was Malcolm Little, who was serving time in prison for robbery. He began writing to Muhammad while he was in prison. Upon his release, Little traveled to Chicago to meet with Muhammad. He quickly persuaded Muhammad that he was serious about joining the Nation of Islam and was given the name Malcolm X.

Just as Muhammad had distinguished himself in the eyes of Fard, Malcolm X became special to Muhammad. Assigned the task of increasing the membership of the NOI, Malcolm X did so with great success. He established Temple No. 7 in New York City and was named its minister.

Membership increased dramatically. The Nation of Islam owned hundreds of acres of land in the Midwest and the South.

By the late 1950s, many former European colonies in Africa were winning their independence and forming new nations. Muhammad sought their financial support whenever he needed more than his own followers could provide.

Had Muhammad been interested in politics, the Nation of Islam could have had a significant influence on American political life. Most of the members of the NOI lived in the North and could vote; they would have voted in any election and for any candidate he backed. But he remained a separatist in his thinking and followed the lead of his mentor, Fard. As Fard had done, Muhammad told his followers not to serve in the U.S. military. In 1942, at the height of World War II, he was convicted of violating the Selective Service Act (the military draft) and served four years in federal prison. Twenty years later, the most famous convert to the Nation of Islam, heavyweight boxer Muhammad Ali (born Cassius Clay), served time in jail for refusing to be drafted to fight in Vietnam.

When Malcolm X made public comments about the assassination of President John F. Kennedy in November 1963, Muhammad "silenced" him. But there was more to the incident. The two men had become increasingly estranged. Muhammad was jealous of Malcolm X's influence. He also may have been worried that Malcolm X would make public the rumors that Muhammad himself had long disobeyed the NOI rules against adultery and had fathered several children out of wedlock.

Malcolm X left the Nation of Islam. He made a pilgrimage to Mecca, the most holy city of world Islam, and upon his return announced that he no longer believed in many of the teachings of the NOI about the evilness of white people. He had discovered that world Islam differed greatly from the NOI. He announced the formation of the Organization of Afro-American Unity. Malcolm X was speaking at an organizational meeting in Harlem in February 1965 when he was assassinated by members of the Nation of Islam.

Muhammad never fully recovered from the split with Malcolm X. Accusations that he had ordered the assassination of his former top

LOUIS FARRAKHAN

The Nation of Islam split into two factions after Elijah Muhammad's death. One faction was led by Wallace Deen Muhammad, the other by Louis Farrakhan. Wallace Deen Muhammad renamed the Nation of Islam the Muslim American Society and tried to adopt religious principles that were closer to world Islam. Farrakhan did not agree with these changes. After three years, he split with Wallace Deen Muhammad.

Farrakhan reformed the Nation of Islam as it had been under Elijah Muhammad, never failing to credit "The Honorable Elijah Muhammad" as the prophet. In fact, under Farrakhan, Elijah Muhammad became godlike to members of the Nation of Islam. Over the next twenty years, Farrakhan's faction far outdistanced the other. Farrakhan continued the creation myth, rules, and separatism that had distinguished the NOI from its beginnings. He built his own power base and following, and made headlines when he led the Million Man March in Washington, D.C., in 1995.

Much had changed in black America since the beginnings of the Nation of Islam. Black people had many more educational and employment opportunities and more awareness of the larger world. Mass communications and the immigration of many Muslims from the Middle East and Indonesia following the relaxation of immigration laws in 1965 helped increase the general level of American knowledge about world Islam.

Faced with overwhelming evidence that some of the basic principles of the Nation of Islam had no foundation in world Islam, Louis Farrakhan finally bowed to the inevitable. Following a bout with prostate cancer, which may have caused him to do some serious soul searching, Farrakhan announced a major change in the official belief system of the Nation of Islam. Whereas the followers of world Islam believe that the founder of Islam, Mohammed, was the last prophet, the Nation of Islam had always taught that W. D. Fard was the Messiah and Elijah Muhammad his prophet. In February 2001, Farrakhan stood side by side on a stage with Wallace Deen Muhammad and declared, "Allah sent Mohammed with the final revelation to the world. . . . There is no prophet after the Prophet Mohammed, and no book after the Koran."[1]

(continued)

minister would not go away, and many people left the Nation. Louis Farrakhan, minister of Temple No. 11 in Boston, became his new lieutenant, struggling for influence with Wallace Deen Muhammad, Elijah Muhammad's son. In poor health in his last years, Elijah Muhammad died in 1975.

H O W A R D
THURMAN

(1900–1981)

✦

Unlike Elijah Muhammad, who allowed his rage over racial injustice to make him hate whites, Howard Thurman found a way to turn hate into love. His writings influenced the leaders of the nonviolent civil rights movement of the mid-twentieth century.

Thurman was born in Daytona, Florida. His father died when he was young, and his mother had to go to work. His grandmother, who had been enslaved, moved in with the family to take care of Howard and his sisters. Thurman's grandmother impressed upon all the children the need to get an education. Although Thurman had to work to help out his family, he kept up with his schooling. In eighth grade, he worked full-time in a dry-cleaning shop but managed to study at night and recite his lessons to the principal of his all-black public school. He was the first black child in the town to earn an eighth-grade certificate.

Daytona was segregated, and the only high school in town was for whites, but Howard was determined to continue his schooling. He had a cousin in Jacksonville, the closest city with a black high school. The cousin offered to take him in and give him one meal a day. A friend gave him a trunk for his belongings. Friends and family raised the money to pay his train fare.

At the train station, Thurman was informed that there was an extra charge to ship his trunk. He did not have the money to pay that charge. He sat down on a bench and put his head in his hands. At that moment, he felt more alone than he ever had before.

A black man, probably a farmer because he was dressed in overalls, had overheard the problem. Without introducing himself to Thurman, he paid the trunk charge, allowing Thurman to board the train to Jacksonville. Sixty-five years later, when Thurman published his autobiography, he dedicated it to "the stranger in the railroad station in Daytona Beach who restored my broken dream sixty-five years ago."[1]

Thurman loved high school and was an excellent student. He later joked that his intelligence was all he had going for him: "It was the only asset I had—I looked terrible!" He had a long face and a very long upper lip, and in repose he looked serious and sad. But he had a ready wit and a fun-loving spirit and was popular with his classmates.

After graduating from high school, Thurman enrolled in Morehouse College in Atlanta, Georgia, where he was a classmate of Martin Luther King Sr. (father of the civil rights leader). He was impressed that the president of Morehouse, John Hope, always referred to the students of the all-male college as "young gentlemen." "Our manhood, and that of our fathers, was denied on all levels by white society," wrote Thurman in his autobiography. "No wonder then that every time Dr. Hope addressed us as 'young gentlemen,' the seeds of self-worth and confidence, long dormant, began to germinate and sprout. The attitudes we developed toward ourselves, as a result of this influence, set Morehouse men apart."[2]

While at Morehouse, Thurman applied for every special program and scholarship he could find and thereby managed to spend summers at Columbia University in New York City. He rented a room in Harlem and managed to live on fifty-five cents a day, feeding his mind with great books. For the first time, he had white classmates, for Columbia was predominantly white. During Thurman's first summer at Columbia, he took what he later considered to be the most important course of his entire education, a course on reflective thinking. It was a basic approach to problem solving that he would use in every aspect of his personal and professional life.

Every Sunday, Thurman attended services at the grand Fifth Avenue Presbyterian Church, whose minister was a Scotsman named Dr. Hugh Black. "The mind of Hugh Black roamed over the vast areas of biblical thought and gave his listeners glad and dramatic tidings from the heart and spirit,"[3] wrote Thurman in his autobiography. Young Howard Thurman wanted to be as learned and as inspiring as Black, and by the time he graduated from Morehouse with honors, he had decided to become a Baptist minister.

Thurman next enrolled at Colgate Rochester Theological Seminary in Rochester, New York. The only African American in the class, he graduated as the top student. He was ordained a minister in 1925. His first pastorate was at Mount Zion Baptist Church in Oberlin, Ohio, where he met and married Kate Kelly, with whom he had a daughter, Olive. Kate died of tuberculosis in 1930. Two years later, Thurman married an old friend, Sue Bailey, who was working for the national Young Women's Christian Association (YWCA). They, too, had a daughter, Anne.

While at Oberlin, Thurman encountered the work of Rufus Jones, a Quaker mystic and leader of the pacifist Interracial Fellowship of Reconciliation. Jones taught at Haverford College in Pennsylvania, and Thurman enrolled at Haverford in order to study with Jones. Thurman was beginning to believe that pacifism might provide a way to fight racial inequality. He was convinced that if black people could overcome their rage at white injustice, they had a chance to win equality.

From 1932 to 1944, Thurman served as dean of Rankin Chapel at

Howard University in Washington, D.C., the most prestigious black college in the nation. During those years, he traveled widely. In 1935, Thurman led a Negro Delegation of Friendship to South Asia, where he met the Indian leader Mohandas Gandhi, called Mahatma, or Great Soul. Gandhi was leading a remarkable movement for Indian independence from England. He taught the use of nonviolent resistance to British rule and by his example inspired thousands of Indians to go to jail rather than be subject to British power. Eventually, England granted independence to India. Thurman was inspired by Gandhi's philosophy of nonviolence and the use of "truth force" in the fight for liberty. He believed that the basis for a similar movement in the United States lay in Christianity.

In 1944, Thurman left Howard University to help the Fellowship of Reconciliation establish the first racially integrated, intercultural church in the United States. The Church for the Fellowship of All Peoples was based in San Francisco, California. Thurman believed that a group united by a common faith in God could be a truth force. He elaborated on his beliefs in a powerful book, *Jesus and the Disinherited*, published in 1949. Thurman stated in his book that the basic goal of Jesus' life was to help the disinherited of the world change from within so that they would be empowered to survive in the face of oppression. He wrote that love rooted in the "deep river of faith" would be powerful enough to overcome oppression. This work would have a strong influence on Martin Luther King Jr. and other future leaders of the civil rights movement.

In 1953, Thurman accepted the post of dean of Marsh Chapel at Boston University. He was the first black dean in the history of Boston University and the first black dean of a major university. He was enlisted by the university to do something similar to what he had done in San Francisco—to create an interracial, interdenominational religious center not only for the campus but for the community as well. The Fellowship Church gave him an indefinite leave of absence, and he promised to return to the West Coast every summer.

Thurman's twelve years at Boston University, 1953–1965, spanned the period of the civil rights movement in the South. He did not participate in the marches and sit-ins and other direct-action efforts to win equal rights for black people, but his writings continued to inform the thinking of the leaders of the movement. Altogether, he wrote twenty books. He had a knack for expressing great truths in eloquent ways, such as:

> There is something in every one of you that waits and listens for the sound of the genuine in yourself. It is the only true guide you will ever have. And if you cannot hear it, you will all of your life spend your days on the ends of strings that somebody else pulls.[4]

The Reverend Dr. Howard Thurman died in 1981.

PART FOUR

LEADERS OF THE CIVIL RIGHTS ERA

ADAM CLAYTON
POWELL JR.

(1908–1972)

◆

Adam Clayton Powell Jr. was born in New Haven, Connecticut, but he was just six months old when his father accepted the position of pastor of Abyssinian Baptist Church and moved his family to New York City. The family included Adam's mother and his sister, Blanche, who was ten years older than he. The Powells settled on the island of Manhattan, where the majority of black people lived in the West 30s to 50s in sections called the Tenderloin and San Juan Hill. By the time the Powells arrived, however, the northern Manhattan neighborhood of Harlem was beginning to open up to black people. The Reverend Powell and other leaders of Abyssinian Baptist Church believed that many black people would soon move to Harlem from the overcrowded tenements of the West Side of Manhattan. They bought land in Harlem and began to build a grand new church on West 138th Street. The new Abyssinian Baptist Church was dedicated when Adam Jr. was fifteen years old.

Although Adam had grown up in the church and listened to his father read him Bible stories at home, he had no interest in following his father into the ministry. In fact, he rebelled against his straight-laced father. All through high school and into college, Adam Jr. was more likely to party and chase after girls than to study. When he began to get serious about his future, he decided he would like to be a doctor. Then late one night in the second half of his senior year in college, he heard a voice say, "Whom shall I send? Who will go for me?"[1] Adam realized that he had been called by God to spread His word. He preached his first sermon in his father's church that spring of 1931, to an assembled congregation of several thousand. Church membership numbered ten thousand by the early 1930s.

While attending Union Theological Seminary and then Teachers College in New York City, Adam served as assistant pastor to his father. Both men soon had more than they could handle as the Great Depression settled in and the largest black church in the country was called upon to help the growing number of poor, jobless people.

Poor people of Harlem suffered greatly. Black people had long been last hired and first fired, which became very evident during the Depression. There was no public assistance (welfare) at that time, and Adam organized a massive relief effort to provide food and used clothing. One day, a group of five black doctors who had been fired from Harlem Hospital sought his help. They had been fired so that five white doctors could have their jobs. Adam formed the Committee on Harlem Hospital and enlisted his parishioners in an effort to picket the hospital, demanding that the black doctors get their jobs back. He was successful in getting the doctors rehired and in bringing about a complete overhaul of the hospital's administration. That experience proved to Adam Clayton Powell Jr. that people could change the conditions under which they lived, if only they worked together and refused to settle for unfair treatment.

In March 1937, a riot occurred in Harlem. It had been sparked by the beating by a white store clerk of a Puerto Rican boy who had shoplifted.

Enraged Harlemites looted stores and set fires, destroying millions of dollars' worth of property. At first, Powell could not understand why the people of Harlem would destroy their own community. Then he began to see that they had done so because it wasn't really theirs. He took a survey of all the businesses along the main shopping street, 125th Street. He found that of five thousand people who worked on that street, only ninety-three were black, and all ninety-three were floor washers and sidewalk sweepers. Not one was a clerk, or a manager, or even a waitress.

Powell enlisted the help of A. Philip Randolph, president of the Brotherhood of Sleeping Car Porters, the nation's largest black union. Together, they organized picket lines outside the major businesses on 125th Street. Their slogan was "Don't buy where you can't work." Black people stayed out of the stores, and soon the stores gave in and began to hire more black people. Powell then took his movement downtown, picketing the major utility company until it, too, agreed to hire more black people.

By 1941, Adam Clayton Powell Jr. was one of the most popular and effective leaders in Harlem. He had a major power base at Abyssinian Baptist Church. In fact, membership in the church had grown so much that on some Sundays parishioners had to be turned away. Powell had loudspeakers installed outside so that his sermons could be heard on the sidewalk.

In September 1941, he declared his candidacy for the city council seat from Harlem. His Sunday morning sermons became political speeches. He won election to the city council. Not long after he took his seat in January 1942, he and three other investors started a newspaper, the *People's Voice*. Powell had a weekly column that he used to rail against lynching, segregation in the military, and job discrimination. The United States had entered World War II after the Japanese attack on the U.S. naval fleet in Pearl Harbor, Hawaii, on December 7, 1941, and Powell was among many black leaders who demanded equal treatment for black servicemen.

In 1942, the New York State legislature changed the U.S. congressional districts so that Harlem became practically its own district. Powell almost immediately announced that he would run for the congressional seat. In the fall of 1944, he won by a huge margin. When he took his seat in Congress, he was the first African American from the North to be a member of the U.S. House of Representatives.

In Congress, Powell fought all the barriers that were placed in front of him—and there were many in Washington, D.C., which was a very southern city. He integrated the congressional dining room and demanded that black reporters be allowed into the congressional gallery. As a member of the House Education and Labor Committee, he tried to introduce bills that would guarantee equal rights for black people, but he was stymied at every turn by southern segregationists.

Eventually, Powell came up with a way to make his point consistently. Every time a bill came before the committee that provided for monies to states or schools, he would attach an equal opportunity clause that became known as the Powell Amendment. Unfortunately, the Powell Amendment never made it to the final bills.

Powell was not well liked in Washington, D.C. Aside from those who hated him because he was black, there were the detractors who criticized his frequent absences, his many trips abroad to attend conferences of African and Asian nations, and his flamboyance. Beginning in 1957, first Abyssinian Baptist Church and then Powell himself were accused of income tax evasion. He charged that it was an underhanded way for the government to get him. Eventually, both Powell and his church were cleared of the charges.

Unlike Powell's colleagues in Congress, the people of Harlem loved him, and they returned him to Washington, D.C., every two years. By 1959, he had been in the House for fifteen years and was the ranking member of the House Education and Labor Committee. When the chairman of the committee retired at the end of that year, and the following year Senator John F. Kennedy of Massachusetts, a Democrat like Powell, won the 1960 presidential election, Powell became the chairman of the committee. He used that powerful position to move important legislation to a vote on the floor of the House. In the first five years of his chairmanship, he successfully guided sixty major laws to passage, including increasing the minimum wage, increasing aid to elementary and secondary education, barring discrimination in salaries paid to women for the same work performed by men, increasing assistance for colleges and universities, increasing job training, implementing juvenile delinquency and youth offenses control, aiding library services, and funding school lunch programs.

Despite all this productivity, Adam Powell was in serious trouble. There was a movement afoot to investigate the finances of his committee and charges that he had put his relatives and friends on the committee payroll, and that he had charged their pleasure trips and his own to the congressional expense account. Plus, he was frequently absent from the floor of Congress. To the charge of absence, Powell pleaded poor health. To the other charges, he responded with his own charge of racism, saying, "I do not do any more than any other member of Congress, and by the Grace of God, I'll not do less."[2] Nevertheless, when Congress convened in January 1967, the House voted 364 to 64 to exclude him.

Although his loyal Harlem constituents reelected him in a special election held to fill his seat, Powell did not return to Congress. He spent most of the next two years on Bimini, an island in the Bahamas, fighting a deep depression that had settled over him. He emerged from that depression two years later, campaigned hard for his old congressional seat, and won. He took the oath of office in January 1969. In July, the U.S. Supreme Court ruled that Congress had acted unconstitutionally in denying him his seat two years earlier.

By the time he ran for reelection, Powell was battling cancer. He faced a tough opponent in Charles B. Rangel, a state assemblyman from Harlem. Rangel won the endorsement of the state Democratic Party and the election.

Powell returned to Bimini and rarely went back to Harlem or even to the United States. After refusing his resignation several times, Abyssinian Baptist Church finally accepted it, with the understanding that he would become pastor emeritus and be available for consultation. He died on Bimini on April 4, 1972. Powell left two sons, both named Adam. Adam III, called Skipper, was his son by his second wife, the pianist Hazel

Scott. Skipper resisted following his father into politics. Adam IV, his son by his third wife, Yvette Flores Diego, did follow in his father's footsteps. He won a seat on the New York City Council and, after serving in that body for two terms, won election to the New York State Assembly. He was unsuccessful in his challenge to Charles Rangel for his father's old congressional seat.

Abyssinian Baptist Church remained a powerful force in Harlem under Powell's successor, the Reverend Calvin Butts. Through a separate corporation, Abyssinian Development Corporation, the church led the rebuilding of Harlem after a long decline in the 1970s and 1980s.

JOSEPH E.
LOWERY

(B . 1 9 2 1)

◆

Joseph E. Lowery was born in Huntsville, Alabama, at a time when white supremacists held sway and black people had no rights. He attended elementary school in Huntsville, then went to Chicago to stay with relatives while he completed middle school. He returned to Huntsville for high school.

Lowery attended Knoxville College in Tennessee before deciding to pursue a theological degree. He studied at Payne College and Theological Seminary in Wilberforce, Ohio, and earned his doctorate of divinity at Chicago Ecumenical Institute.

In 1952, Lowery accepted the position of pastor of Warren Street United Methodist Church in Mobile, Alabama. It was a time of considerable unrest among southern black people. For one thing, the southern economic base had changed from agriculture to industry. For another, many whites maintained their identity at the expense of black people; that is, as long as they had black people to look down on, they were "somebody" in their own eyes.

The United States had just been victorious in World War II. Many black men had fought in Europe in World War II and had distinguished themselves for their bravery. But they returned home to find the same old segregation and lack of opportunity that they had left behind. Lowery, who had seen a different life in Chicago, was determined to lead his fellow black Mobile residents in a crusade against segregation. With others, he formed the Alabama Civic Affairs Association, whose purpose was to desegregate local buses and public places like movie theaters and restaurants.

Similar activity was taking place in Montgomery, Alabama. In early December 1955, after Rosa Parks, an African American seamstress, was arrested for refusing to give up her bus seat to a white man, the black citizens of Montgomery began a boycott of the city buses. They formed the Montgomery Improvement Association and elected as its president the Reverend Martin Luther King Jr., the young minister of Dexter Avenue Baptist Church.

Joseph Lowery was excited by the possibilities of the boycott and traveled to Montgomery to help out. He assisted in organizing taxi brigades and vans to transport people to work and to keep the boycotters' spirits up by exhorting them to keep fighting for principle. In spite of threats and bombings—Martin Luther King Jr.'s home was bombed—the boycott prevailed. More than a year after Rosa Parks's arrest, the U.S. Supreme Court ruled segregation on public transportation illegal.

In 1957, Lowery and other southern black ministers formed the Southern Christian Leadership Conference (SCLC) to press for black civil rights in the South. Martin Luther King Jr. was president. Lowery was named vice president. Their first major action was a prayer vigil to Washington, D.C. Lowery took part in all the major actions undertaken by the SCLC. In 1965, he was among the leaders of the Selma to

Montgomery March, guiding the delegation that took the marchers' demands for voting rights to Alabama Governor George Wallace.

After Dr. Martin Luther King Jr. was assassinated in 1968, Lowery tried to hold the SCLC together, assisting Dr. King's chief aide, the Reverend Ralph David Abernathy. Lowery himself became president of the SCLC in 1977. He led the organization in campaigns for economic rights, negotiating with major companies to hire more African Americans and promoting opportunities for minority-owned companies. He also helped establish the Black Leadership Forum to "promote creative and coordinated Black Leadership, diverse in membership but clear on its priority, to empower African Americans to improve their own lives and to expand their opportunities to fully participate in American social, economic and political life."[1]

In the 1980s and 1990s, Lowery focused on international relations, protesting apartheid in South Africa and leading peace delegations to the Middle East and Central America. He understood, however, that racism and discrimination continued in the southern United States, and he maintained his vigilance in that arena. He helped desegregate public facilities in Nashville, Tennessee, and campaigned for the hiring of black police officers in Birmingham, Alabama.

All the while, Lowery served as pastor for several different churches. He retired from the pulpit in 1997 and from the SCLC in 1998. He continued his activism, emphasizing the importance of African American voting. He helped bring about the extension of provisions to the Voting Rights Act of 2007. The years did not soften his outspokenness. In 2006, at the funeral of Coretta Scott King, with President George W. Bush in the audience, he asserted of the war in Iraq, "We know now there were no weapons of mass destruction over there. But Coretta knew and we know that there are weapons of misdirection right down here. Millions without health insurance. Poverty abounds. For war billions more but no more for the poor!"[2]

In December 2001, as part of Lowery's eightieth birthday celebration, the city of Atlanta, Georgia, renamed Ashby Street as Joseph E. Lowery Boulevard.

MALCOLM

X

(1925–1965)

✦

Malcolm X was probably the most famous example of the great appeal of the Nation of Islam (NOI) to African American prisoners. When he joined the NOI, he was serving a ten-year prison sentence for burglary.

Born Malcolm Little in Lansing, Michigan, on May 19, 1925, he was one of eight children. His father, Earl Little, was a Baptist minister and a devoted follower of Marcus Garvey, a black nationalist who had come to the United States from his native Jamaica. Garvey had attracted a wide following among black Americans with his determination to wrest control of Africa from European colonial powers. To this end, he urged African Americans to return to Africa.

Malcolm Little's hometown of Lansing, Michigan, harbored a strong white supremacist movement. One organization, the Black Legion, targeted Malcolm's father for his outspoken black nationalist views. Death threats against the Reverend Little from the Black Legion forced the Littles to move twice before Malcolm was four years old. In 1929, when Malcolm was four, the family home was burned to the ground. Malcolm had just started first grade when his father was run over by a streetcar—murdered, it was rumored, by the Black Legion.

When Malcolm was fourteen, his mother, Louise, was declared insane and committed to the state mental hospital. He was sent to live with his older half-sister in Boston, where he told people he was from Detroit because no one seemed to have heard of Lansing, Michigan. His reddish hair and complexion prompted his new friends to nickname him Detroit Red. Malcolm tried to get jobs in Boston, and later in Harlem, but there were few opportunities for a young man with little schooling and a lot of anger toward white society over what his family had suffered. He got involved in petty crime, graduated to more serious activities, and was convicted and sentenced to prison for armed robbery. At the lowest point in his young life, Malcolm was visited by his brother Reginald, who told him about the preaching of a man named Elijah Muhammad in Chicago.

Intrigued by what his brother had told him about the Nation of Islam (NOI), Malcolm began to read all he could. He wanted to write to Elijah Muhammad, leader of the NOI, but his lack of education embarrassed him. Determined to educate himself, he copied the entire dictionary in order to teach himself the words he needed to write a letter. He also began to follow Elijah Muhammad's dictates about clean living and became a model prisoner. In 1952, after serving six and a half years of his ten-year sentence, he was paroled.

As soon as he was able, Malcolm traveled to Chicago to meet with Elijah Muhammad, who gave him the last name X to replace his slave name (Little). The X signified lack of knowledge of his true African name. Malcolm X was eager to help spread the word and attract more converts to the Nation of Islam, and he proved to be a powerful and charismatic organizer. By 1954, he was the minister of Temple No. 7 in Harlem, and by the late 1950s, according to one estimate, he had almost single-handedly increased the membership of the NOI from five hundred to more than twenty-five thousand. Minister Malcolm X was the most famous Black Muslim in America.

In 1959, Malcolm X was featured in a week-long television special called "The Hate That Hate Produced." As its title indicated, the program suggested that racial hatred on the part of whites had led to the separatism and hatred of whites that were major pillars of the Nation of Islam. The program also tracked the emergence of Malcolm X as one of the NOI's most important leaders.

Racial tensions were high during the late 1950s and early 1960s. Southern black people, led by their ministers and often aided by northern blacks and whites, engaged in direct-action tactics, such as marches, sit-ins, and boycotts, to challenge the segregation laws. In response, white segregationists often attacked, beat, and even killed demonstrators. J. Edgar Hoover, the longtime director of the Federal Bureau of Investigation (FBI), became convinced that the peace of the nation was at risk. FBI agents began to infiltrate the southern movements as well as other black organizations. The FBI also infiltrated the NOI, monitoring its phone calls and meetings with wiretaps, bugs, and secret cameras. One agent even acted as Malcolm X's bodyguard.

Elijah Muhammad worried that Malcolm X was becoming too powerful. He also worried that Malcolm X was too political. He had always believed that the NOI should refrain from political activity in order to prevent government interference. He suspected FBI infiltration in his organization and worried about it.

For his part, Malcolm X had ceased to revere his mentor. He had received confirmation of troubling rumors that had surfaced by the late 1950s. Elijah Muhammad had broken his own rules against adultery and had fathered several children out of wedlock. Malcolm X lost all respect for the man whom he had considered a father figure and began to consider ways to take control of the NOI.

The eventual cause of the break between the two men was a statement that Malcolm X made after President John F. Kennedy was assassinated in November 1963. Malcolm X said it was a case of the chickens coming home to roost, by which he meant that the hatred in America had claimed America's own president. But many people took it to mean that President Kennedy had got what was coming to him, and there was a great outcry against Malcolm X over that statement. Elijah Muhammad seized the opportunity to silence his top minister.

Rather than endure the period of silence that had been imposed on him, Malcolm X left the Nation of Islam. He went on a pilgrimage to Mecca in Saudi Arabia, which all practicing Muslims are supposed to do at least once in their lifetime. He learned during his travels that the version of Islam taught by the NOI was very different from world Islam, which is a religion of many races. Malcolm X concluded that it was not American whites who were evil but their society. When he returned to the United States, he formed the Organization of Afro-American Unity (OAAU), which did not deny membership to white people who supported his cause.

Before Malcolm X could build his new organization, however, he was himself assassinated in 1965 by members of the Nation of Islam. The OAAU withered without him. But Malcolm X's reputation and his message grew greater as the years passed. He became revered for his charisma and his courage and for having a faith so deep that he could lift himself up from criminality to become a respected and powerful leader of his people.

KING JR.

(1929–1968)

✦

The most towering figure in the civil rights movement, Martin Luther King Jr. was born into a church family. His father, the Reverend Martin Luther King Sr., was pastor of Ebenezer Baptist Church in Atlanta, Georgia. The Kings thus had deep roots in Atlanta and enjoyed great respect in Atlanta's black community. The Reverend King was a proud, dignified man who taught his children, "You are as good as anybody else," and who refused to bow to the segregation practices of the time.

Young Martin was an excellent student and entered Morehouse College in Atlanta when he was only fifteen years old. The family assumed he would follow his father into the ministry, but he wasn't so sure. He had heard all of his father's sermons, and it seemed to young

Martin that the older man, in spite of his own pride, was using the pulpit to advise his parishioners to put up with the indignities of southern life. Martin could not see himself exhorting his parishioners to love God and be patient with the burdens placed upon them.

But one of Martin's professors at Morehouse, Dr. Benjamin Mays, believed he would make a fine minister. Dr. Mays told Martin that he could be an intellectual minister and preach sermons based on his deep study of the Bible and history. He reminded Martin that the church was the power center of the black community, the place where the greatest number of people could be influenced at one time. When Martin told his parents that he had decided to become a minister, they were overjoyed.

Martin enrolled at Crozier Theological Seminary in Chester, Pennsylvania. He learned about Mohandas K. Gandhi and his nonviolent protests against the British in India. Gandhi bade his followers not to fight back, even against violence. They would win by "truth force." It took many years, but eventually Indians won their independence from Great Britain in 1947 by persistently demonstrating against British rule and going to jail in droves.

After graduating from Crozier, King did post-graduate work at Boston University. In Boston he met Coretta Scott, a student at the New England Conservatory of Music. She was from Alabama and had no intention of returning to the South to live. But Martin won her over. They were married not long after he received his degree in theology. He then accepted an invitation to be the pastor of Dexter Avenue Baptist Church in Montgomery, Alabama, the same church that the Reverend Vernon Johns had pastored. Martin and Coretta had barely settled into their new life in Montgomery when the boycott of the city's buses following the arrest of Rosa Parks catapulted the twenty-six-year-old minister to fame.

A group of black people in the city formed the Montgomery Improvement Association (MIA) to aid the boycott by arranging for alternative transportation, raising money to buy vans and print leaflets, and to publicize the boycott. Martin Luther King Jr. was elected president of the MIA. King traveled around the country speaking against segregation and raising money. He exhorted black Montgomeryites to stay off the buses even if it meant losing their jobs or walking miles to work. His house was bombed; he received death threats; but he refused to back down. He believed that the same "truth force" that had been successful in India could be made to work against southern segregation. More than a year later, the U.S. Supreme Court ruled that segregation on public transportation was illegal.

King did not want to lose the momentum of the boycott. He wanted to harness the "truth force" to bring about more civil rights for black people in the South. With other southern ministers, he formed the Southern Christian Leadership Conference (SCLC) with a plan to press for voting rights for black people. King resigned his pastorship at Dexter Avenue Baptist Church in order to devote himself to the work of the SCLC.

The winds of change were blowing throughout the South. Barely had King organized the SCLC when groups of college students began to sit in at lunch counters in Greensboro, North Carolina, and Nashville, Tennessee. The students formed their own group, with the help of the SCLC, calling it the Student Nonviolent Coordinating Committee (SNCC, pronounced "Snick"). As the name suggests, they, too, followed the philosophy of nonviolence and won the right to eat at public lunch counters. They then started going on Freedom Rides in the South to test new laws against segregation on interstate transportation and to conduct voter registration drives in Mississippi and other parts of the South.

Martin Luther King Jr. and the SCLC supported these efforts and pursued their own. In Birmingham, Alabama, leading an effort to desegregate public facilities in that city, King was arrested and jailed. Although his advisers said the movement needed him to be free, he believed he had to set an example, as Mohandas Gandhi had done in India. While he was in the Birmingham jail, King wrote an open letter to his fellow clergymen—both the black clergymen in the city who had not joined in the protests, and the white clergymen who had issued a public plea to the black people of Birmingham not to join the demonstrations. His letter explained the reasons for the campaign and defended the direct-action tactics, such as marches and sit-ins and other demonstrations. The letter also reminded the ministers of their own responsibility to uphold justice and fight injustice.

Despite all the publicity over the demonstrations by SNCC, the SCLC, and other civil rights organizations, the number of people who directly participated in the civil rights movement was very small—less than 5 percent of the nation's black population. In Birmingham, the black adults did not get involved until their children tried to demonstrate and were mowed down with fire hoses and police dogs. When thousands and thousands of black people marched through the streets of Birmingham and millions of Americans watched scenes of police brutality on television, the business leaders of Birmingham were ready to compromise.

Gradually, the tide turned. More and more people joined the movement to demand equal rights for black people. In August 1963, more than two hundred thousand people of all races converged on Washington, D.C., in the March for Jobs and Freedom, and to pressure President Kennedy to introduce a strong civil rights bill. The leaders of the six major civil rights organizations shared a podium set up in front of the Lincoln Memorial. Of all the speeches, King's was the most stirring and the most memorable. "I have a dream," King intoned. "It is a dream deeply rooted in the American dream. I have a dream that one day this nation will rise up and live out the true meaning of its creed: 'We hold these truths to be self-evident, that *all* men are created equal.'"[1]

Less than two months later, President John F. Kennedy was assassinated in Dallas, Texas. His successor, Vice President Lyndon B. Johnson of Texas, promised to follow through on the late president's intention to introduce a strong civil rights bill, and the Civil Rights Act of 1964 made good on Johnson's promise. That same year, Martin Luther King Jr. was awarded the Nobel Peace Prize, an international prize given by the Norwegian Parliament. King was only the second African American to win the prize. The award to King was a big boost to the civil rights movement. It proved better than any other gesture that the rest of the world was keenly aware of the struggle in the United States and supported the black people of America.

In the summer of 1965, rioting in northern cities caused King to realize that while he and other leaders had been concentrating on winning equal rights for southern black people, they had overlooked the poor, disenfranchised black population of the North. He tried to bring the nonviolent direct-action tactics that had worked so well in the South to Chicago, but he failed to convince the majority of black Chicagoans that their lives would be significantly improved through nonviolent demonstrations.

At about the same time, the leaders of the Student Nonviolent Coordinating Committee (SNCC) forswore nonviolence. During the summer of 1964, while trying to register black voters in Mississippi, SNCC workers had been beaten and arrested again and again. Four young men had been murdered. SNCC issued a call for black power and criticized the older civil rights leaders as has-beens.

Martin Luther King Jr. was not ready to be a has-been. He had for many years been thinking about enlarging the scope of his nonviolent philosophy, applying it not just to the human rights struggle of black people in the United States but to the cause of world peace. He began to speak out against U.S. involvement in the war in Vietnam. He also began to plan a massive Poor People's March on Washington in the spring of 1968.

When striking black sanitation workers in Memphis, Tennessee, appealed to King to join them to support their cause, he didn't want to take time away from the planning of his Poor People's March. But he realized that there was great potential for violence in Memphis, and he believed he could buttress the nonviolent intentions of the strike leaders, so he went there to help. He was assassinated in Memphis on April 4, 1968. He was not yet forty years old.

Although the Reverend Martin Luther King Jr. lived only forty years, he changed the course of American history. His deep faith and his belief in the power of nonviolent action to overcome injustice had a profound effect on the life of his nation and the world. He is regarded as one of the most important figures of the twentieth century.

ANDREW J.
YOUNG

(B. 1932)

✦

Andrew Young was born in New Orleans, Louisiana. His grandfather had been a successful businessman who had operated a drugstore, a pool hall, and a saloon. His father was a dentist. The Youngs were among the elite of the city's black population, which was largely poor and uneducated. Dr. Young could have afforded to live in a well-to-do white neighborhood, but no one would sell to him. Andrew and his brother, Walter, grew up in an integrated but poor neighborhood where their early playmates were Irish and Italian as well as black.

When it was time for the Young children to enroll in school, they learned about segregation. They went to a black school, while their white playmates went to a white school. As they grew older and could ride their bicycles down to the city park, they learned that they were not allowed in the park because they were black.

The Youngs were active in Central Congregational Church. When Andrew was old enough, he worked with younger children in the Sunday school and sang in the youth choir. But he had no plans to become a minister. His father wanted him to be a doctor or a dentist.

Andrew attended a private high school in New Orleans, then enrolled at Dillard University in New Orleans for a year before transferring to Howard University in Washington, D.C., where his father had studied. Young majored in biology, but he really didn't want to go into medicine. Upon graduation from Howard in May 1951, he had no idea what he wanted to do.

A series of events that summer helped point him to his future path. His parents drove him back to New Orleans from Washington, D.C. There were few hotels or motels on the way that would accept black people, so they spent one night at a religious camp in King's Mountain, North Carolina, where Andrew met a young white minister who was preparing to do missionary work in Africa. Andrew had had very little contact with whites in general, and meeting a white minister who was not racist was a revelation. Back home, he met the new minister of Central Congregational Church and accompanied him to another religious camp in Brownsville, Texas, where he met more young southern white people who had overcome their racist upbringing. He decided that there must be more to religion than he had thought and that he should study for the ministry.

Andrew enrolled at Hartford Seminary in Connecticut and upon graduation was ordained a minister in the Congregational Church. He married Jean Childs, a young woman he had met while working one summer in Alabama, and accepted the position of pastor of a church in Thomasville, Georgia. He encouraged his parishioners to register to vote and was the object of a Ku Klux Klan protest as a result. Offered a job in the Department of Youth at the headquarters of the National Council of Churches in New York City, Andrew Young moved his wife and two small daughters north.

Meanwhile, the direct-action civil rights movement had gotten under-way in the South. The Montgomery Bus Boycott occurred while the Youngs were in Thomasville; but the student sit-ins at lunch counters and the formation of the Student Nonviolent Coordinating Committee (SNCC) took place while they were in New York. So did the Freedom Rides. The young couple watched television coverage of the beatings of the Freedom Riders and the burning of the interstate buses, asking themselves how they could possibly remain in New York when they belonged in the South.

Coincidentally, shortly afterward, Young was offered a job managing a United Church of Christ voter registration drive in Alabama. He jumped at the chance, moved his family to Alabama, and soon joined the Southern Christian Leadership Conference (SCLC), the organization of ministers that Martin Luther King Jr., Joseph Lowery, and others had founded in 1957. He quickly became one of King's most trusted advisers. He was a superb organizer, he was very good with young people, and he was successful dealing with white people.

Young showed his talents in the spring of 1963 when the SCLC decided to desegregate the city of Birmingham, Alabama. The campaign began with a number of small peaceful marches. When the white author-ities realized what was happening, they started arresting the leaders. Martin Luther King Jr. was among those who went to jail. When six small children presented themselves to Young as volunteers, he told them that they were too young to go to jail, but they could go to the whites-only public library. The children marched straight to the nearest white library, headed for the children's room, and sat down to read. The librarian was aghast but made no move to evict the children.

The young black people of Birmingham were far more willing than most of the adults to demonstrate for their freedom. Urged on by Young and another of his aides, James Bevel, King called an assembly at Birmingham's Sixteenth Street Baptist Church, and nearly a thousand young people showed up to hear him talk about nonviolent protest. They then formed orderly lines and marched solemnly through down-town Birmingham. This Children's Crusade was a great story for the media, which covered it widely.

The following day, more than a thousand young people set off from Sixteenth Street Baptist Church to march downtown. This time, the police and firemen were waiting for them. They turned powerful fire hoses on the marchers, smashing small bodies against fences and sidewalks. Then they set police dogs on them, snarling and snapping and dragging them about. Television cameras recorded it all, and that night in their living rooms, millions of Americans were presented with a sight they would never forget. Satellites carried the shocking images around the world. Birmingham, Alabama, became an international scandal.

Andrew Young knew it was time to contact the most powerful white businessmen in Birmingham. These men understood that Birmingham's reputation was at stake and that their businesses would suffer. Three days after the hoses and dogs were set upon Birmingham's young black people, a biracial agreement was reached under which public accommodations would be desegregated, job opportunities would be increased, and all those arrested in the demonstrations would be freed.

By 1964, Andrew Young was executive director of the SCLC. Young helped plan and strategize the Selma, Alabama, voter registration drive, the Selma to Montgomery March, and other demonstrations. He accompanied Martin Luther King Jr. to Oslo, Norway, to receive the Nobel Peace Prize. After the 1964 Civil Rights Act and the 1965 Voting Rights Act were signed into law by President Lyndon B. Johnson, putting in place the basic legal structure for guaranteeing equal rights to black people, Young helped try to find another cause for the SCLC. After all, black people in the northern cities had not been touched at all by the gains of the civil rights movement in the South. But efforts to bring the tactics and philosophy of nonviolent protest to a northern city like Chicago were unsuccessful.

During 1966 and 1967, there were major riots in Cleveland, Ohio; Jackson, Mississippi; Boston, Massachusetts; Tampa, Florida; Cincinnati, Ohio, Newark, New Jersey; Hartford, Connecticut; Philadelphia, Pennsylvania; and many other cities. Leaders of the SCLC and other major civil rights organizations issued an appeal to end the riots, but the violence continued. It was not a movement that could be controlled but a disorganized and destructive expression of anger and frustration. It occurred to Young and others in the SCLC leadership that the urban rioters had rioted not so much because they were poor and black and discriminated against as because they were poor and discriminated against. They decided to take up the cause of the poor, whatever their race, and made plans for the Poor People's March on Washington in April 1968.

Young was standing next to Martin Luther King Jr. on the balcony of the Lorraine Motel in Memphis, Tennessee, when King was felled by an assassin's bullet. In the aftermath of his friend's death, Young and the other leaders of the SCLC scrambled to regroup and to continue plans for the Poor People's March on Washington. All the while, they knew that King's death meant the end of an era—the end of the nonviolent civil rights movement. Looking back on those turbulent years, Young would say, "It was probably the happiest time of my life. It was rough, but the issues were very clear-cut. We knew what we had to do and we had a group of people pretty much committed to doing it."[1]

Looking to his own future, Young decided that the next important arena for black people was the political one. They had won the right to vote; now they must use it to bring about needed changes in the South. In 1970, he ran for the Georgia Fifth District congressional seat but lost to a white candidate in that predominantly white district. Two years later, the lines of the district were redrawn, with the result that more black voters were within its boundaries. Young ran again for the congressional seat, and this time he won. He was the first black congressman to be elected from the South since Reconstruction. He was reelected in 1974.

In the 1976 presidential campaign, Young supported his fellow Georgian, Jimmy Carter, the first nationally known elected official to do so. He campaigned for him across the country and got to know him well. Shortly after Carter was elected, the new president selected Andrew Young as U.S. ambassador to the United Nations. Since the president had decided to make that position a cabinet post, Young became the first African American in history to have a cabinet-level position.

Most black politicians—and most of Young's friends—urged him not to accept the appointment. They believed he could help African

Americans more by remaining in Congress. Some went so far as to charge that the appointment was a "political kidnapping," planned by Georgia's political power structure to retake control of Atlanta.

Young wasn't sure he should take the post, and he thought long and hard about it before he made his decision. He had long been interested in foreign affairs, especially in the newly independent nations of Africa. He believed that racism played a big role on the international stage as well as on the American one, that "white people are afraid of black people, and black people—maybe for good reasons—don't trust white people and, more important, don't understand them. Maybe the single most important dynamic in today's foreign relations is racism."[2] Andrew Young had a lot of experience as a "reconciler of men," and he believed he could be an effective ambassador.

Ambassador Young took up his new post on January 29, 1977. He approached this job in the same way as he had approached his civil rights work. "I hate to blame everything I do on God," he once said, but he believed that God would have approved of his approach, which was to look at situations and say honestly what he felt. He traveled widely, paid more attention to the independent nations of Africa than any of his predecessors, and made many friends abroad.

Some of his statements about world affairs made headlines and incurred criticism. But President Carter stood by him until 1979, when Young had a secret meeting with a representative of the Palestinian Liberation Organization (PLO). Carter himself had been trying to find a way to make peace between Israel and the Occupied Territories (Palestine). But he was most displeased that his ambassador took it upon himself to enter the discussion. It was against U.S. policy to negotiate with the PLO, and when Young's explanation of why he had taken the meeting was evasive, Carter had no choice but to ask him to resign. Young submitted his resignation in September 1979, after two and a half years at the United Nations. Two years later, in January 1981, President Carter awarded Andrew Young the Presidential Medal of Freedom, the nation's highest civilian honor.

JAMES L. BEVEL (B. 1936)

James Luther Bevel was a chief architect of the
Children's Crusade in Birmingham, Alabama, which
helped turn the tide of public opinion against the violent
resistance to the civil rights movement and enabled
Andrew J. Young to negotiate with Birmingham's business leaders.

Bevel was born in Itta Bena, Mississippi. After serving in the army, he was called to the ministry and
enrolled in the American Baptist Theological Seminary
in Nashville, Tennessee. Nashville had several black col-
leges, so it was a natural breeding ground for the black student movement that was
forming in the late 1950s. Bevel joined the Nashville chapter of the newly formed
Southern Christian Leadership Conference (SCLC), but he was eager for greater
activism than the organization of southern Baptist ministers favored.

Other Nashville students agreed. Many of them joined the Nashville Christian
Leadership Council (NCLC), founded in 1958 by the Reverend Kelly Miller Smith of
First Baptist Church. In 1959, some NCLC members underwent training in nonviolent resistance provided by the Reverend James Lawson. In addition to Bevel, the
group included John Lewis and Diane Nash.

The NCLC organized sit-ins against Nashville's segregated lunch counters.
Simultaneously, a group of students in Greensboro, North Carolina, began sitting
in at a Woolworth's lunch counter. The Nashville students and the Greensboro students later helped to form the Student Nonviolent Coordinating Committee (SNCC,
pronounced "Snick").

As chairman of the NCLC, Bevel participated in the Freedom Rides to desegregate interstate travel and public accommodations in the South. He headed up the
SCLC's Mississippi Project for voting rights in 1962. The following year, after
Dr. Martin Luther King Jr. was jailed in Birmingham, he went to that city to help
reinvigorate the desegregation campaign there. He was the primary architect of the
Children's Crusade, leading the young black people of the city to march through
the streets.

(continued)

JAMES L. BEVEL *(continued)*

Bevel helped plan the 1963 March on Washington and the 1965 Selma to Montgomery March. He and Diane Nash had married, and Dr. King awarded the couple the SCLC's highest honor in 1965, the Rosa Parks Award. Bevel then worked in the SCLC's campaign against segregated housing in Chicago, in support of the Memphis sanitation workers in 1968, and in the Poor People's Campaign that the SCLC pursued after the assassination of Dr. Martin Luther King Jr.

In 1969, Bevel left the SCLC and settled in Chicago, where his wife had been born. They later divorced, but he remained in the city. He became pastor of the Hebraic-Christian-Islamic Assembly in Chicago and worked as an adviser to the Nation of Islam. In 1992, he ran for vice president on a ticket with Lyndon LaRouche, a perennial third-party presidential candidate with extreme right-wing views. Because of his shifting allegiances, Bevel has been described as an opportunist by some. Others assert that he simply seeks justice for his people and is willing to work with whoever can help make that happen.

Young and his wife, Jean, returned to Atlanta after he left his UN post. Within a year, he had decided to run for mayor of that city. He won election in October 1981 and won again in 1985. At the time he became mayor, Atlanta was in a severe economic recession. He worked hard to attract international investment to the city and managed to improve the economy considerably. He was also successful in persuading the International Olympic Committee to hold the 1996 summer games in Atlanta.

In 1990, Young was unsuccessful in his bid for the governorship of Georgia. In 2004, he considered a run for the Senate from Georgia; but he decided not to reenter public life. In 1996, Young and two partners formed Good Works International. Originally aimed at fostering long-term economic development in Africa and the Caribbean by arranging partnerships with American companies, the firm has also represented American companies in their operations both at home and abroad.

As the public face of the partnership, Young has continued to take controversial positions. Under contract to Wal-Mart to improve its employee relations, he acknowledged that employees of the giant discount store chain received low pay and few benefits, but defended the store's record of diversity in hiring and its willingness to open stores in poor neighborhoods. He went too far, however, when he publicly criticized immigrant owners of small grocery stores who exploited black customers by being rude to them and overcharging them. A Wal-Mart spokeswoman expressed dismay that a man who had worked so hard for equal rights in America could make such remarks, and Good Works International lost the Wal-Mart contract.

Despite such criticisms, Young's reputation as a man of peace and self-control remains largely intact. He serves on the boards of many organizations, including the National Peace Foundation, the Children's Scholarship Fund, and Operation Hope, a group that teaches financial literacy to young people. He is also a professor at Georgia State University's Andrew Young School of Policy Studies.

LEWIS

(B. 1940)

✦

In contrast to James Bevel, John Lewis has never wavered from the non-violent, mainstream southern Baptist path. He was born in rural Alabama, the son of sharecroppers. His family were churchgoers and hard workers, and the little boy's life revolved around work and church. Everyone in the family had to work as soon as he or she was old enough, and when John was five years old, he was put in charge of his family's chickens. He took his responsibilities very seriously. He loved those chickens, gave them each a name, and preached to them at night to keep them quiet. His habit of giving sermons in the chicken coop earned him the nickname "Preacher."

When he was old enough to understand what segregation meant, John Lewis felt a deep sense of injustice. He knew that segregation was wrong, that he and his family and other people of color did not deserve to be denied the same rights as white people. But his parents counseled him to accept what could not be changed. "Don't make trouble," they said. "Don't get in the way."

Then one day when he was fifteen, he heard the voice of Dr. Martin Luther King Jr. on the radio. Dr. King was speaking about the Montgomery Bus Boycott, which was then in progress. The black people of Montgomery were staying off the city buses to protest segregation. Young John Lewis was inspired by Dr. King's words, so he decided, in his own small way, to "make some trouble." He marched into the Pike County Public Library and politely requested a library card. He was not surprised to hear the librarian tell him that the library was for whites only. He went home and wrote the library a letter of protest.

After graduating from high school, Lewis wanted to attend Troy State University, close to home. But Troy State was segregated. He was accepted at American Baptist Theological Seminary in Nashville, Tennessee. Lewis wrote to Dr. King, telling the minister how he had been inspired by him and telling him that he wanted to try to integrate Troy State. Dr. King sent Lewis a Greyhound bus ticket.

In the summer of 1957, Lewis rode to Montgomery, Alabama, and met his hero. Dr. King and his aides promised to help Lewis try to get into Troy State, but Dr. King warned him that he would be putting not only his own safety at risk but also that of his family. Lewis believed he was doing the right thing, but as his parents expressed their fears to him—that his father would lose his job driving a school bus, that they might have to get off the land on which they farmed—he decided he could not put them in danger. He gave up on his plans to attend Troy State and returned to Nashville.

When Lewis got back to Nashville, he sensed a new air of urgency and purpose among the students—the sense that the civil rights movement needed the involvement of young people. Someone came up with the slogan "Free by '63," and it rippled throughout the college town of Nashville. Lewis came under the influence of James Lawson. Born in Pennsylvania in 1928, Lawson had joined the Fellowship of

Reconciliation, an interracial group committed to peace and social justice. He had done missionary work in India and had studied the principles of Mohandas K. Gandhi. Upon his return to the United States, he had met Martin Luther King Jr., who had also studied Gandhi's philosophy. King urged Lawson to move to the South and join the movement. Lawson enrolled at divinity school at Vanderbilt University in Nashville, where he also served as southern director of the Fellowship of Reconciliation and conducted workshops in nonviolence for the Southern Christian Leadership Conference (SCLC). John Lewis attended those workshops.

Lewis was drawn to Lawson's teachings about the nonviolent way of life—that it wasn't simply a tactic but a way of being. As Lewis wrote, "This sense of love, this sense of peace, the capacity for compassion, is something you carry inside yourself every waking minute of the day."[1] After months of attending SCLC workshops, John and a group of other students staged their first sit-in at the lunch counter of a downtown department store. Their plan was to wage a full-blown campaign on downtown Nashville, and they demonstrated against six downtown stores for three months. On May 10, 1960, those stores began to serve black customers.

John Lewis paid a price for that victory. Along with the others, he had been arrested for violating the segregation laws. His parents were shocked and dismayed. They told him that he was supposed to be studying, not sitting in, not being arrested. Although his activities put them in no danger, they were embarrassed and fearful for his safety. A deep rift had formed between Lewis and his parents that would take many years to heal. From that time on, he considered his fellows in the civil rights movement his family.

The SCLC stepped in to organize the unorganized, spontaneous student sit-in movement, in Nashville and elsewhere, and the Student Nonviolent Coordinating Committee (SNCC, pronounced "Snick") was born. Officially launched in April 1960, SNCC sought to coordinate the use of nonviolent direct action to attack segregation and other forms of racism. The students were young, committed, and almost fearless in their willingness to take risks for what they believed. The Interstate Commerce Commission (ICC) had ruled in 1955 that public facilities on interstate transportation routes could not be segregated. In 1961, SNCC and CORE (Congress of Racial Equality), another civil rights organization, decided to test the ICC ruling by staging a series of Freedom Rides on interstate buses. John Lewis was among those chosen for the first Freedom Rides. The protesters, both black and white, gathered in Washington, D.C., then boarded a southbound Greyhound bus. At each stop, they entered the terminal and used the facilities.

The trip had little incident until Rock Hill, North Carolina, where the Freedom Riders were approaching the whites-only waiting room when a group of white men attacked them. Lewis was beaten, but he refused to press charges when the police finally showed up to restore order. A telegram reached him in Rock Hill, inviting him to Philadelphia to interview for an overseas missionary job. He left the Freedom Ride, promising to return as soon as he could. While he was gone, the Greyhound bus on which he had been riding was attacked and burned in Aniston, Alabama.

Twelve riders suffering from smoke inhalation were taken to a nearby hospital, but only one, a white female, was admitted. The hospital was for whites only. Lewis hastened to rejoin the Freedom Ride. This time, the group departed from Nashville, bound for Birmingham, where they were beaten, arrested, and jailed. Released on bail, they boarded another bus bound for Montgomery. The six Freedom Riders were the only passengers on the bus. No one else wanted to risk being beaten, and it was hard for Greyhound to find drivers willing to put their own lives on the line.

When the bus pulled into the Montgomery depot, the Freedom Riders had an eerie sense that they were all alone. The place was almost deserted. The riders debarked hesitantly. Then, out of nowhere, dozens of people appeared from every direction, carrying every makeshift weapon imaginable. Crying "Git them niggers," they fell upon the Freedom Riders, clubbing and beating them. Television cameras and reporters also appeared and were attacked. John Lewis was knocked out when someone swung a Coca-Cola crate against his head. Others were so severely beaten that they had to be hospitalized.

Robert F. Kennedy, attorney general of the United States and brother of President John F. Kennedy, finally demanded that the governor of Alabama send in the National Guard, which took up positions along the bus route. And now the Freedom Riders had other reinforcements. Students were flooding into Montgomery from all across the South and from as far north as Washington, D.C. Dozens of interstate buses would pass through the South that summer carrying integrated groups of Freedom Riders, and John Lewis had decided he could not be a missionary in India. His mission was to stay in the South and continue the fight for equal rights.

The Freedom Rides marked a shift in the temperature of the direct-action civil rights movement, an increased aggressiveness, an intention to provoke. The outrage generated by the violent resistance to the Freedom Rides swelled the movement with new members, mostly college students, both black and white. John Lewis was elected to the SNCC executive committee and also to the board of the SCLC. He was still taking courses in Nashville, but he was carrying a light academic load in order to devote as much time as possible to the movement.

He was participating in the Birmingham, Alabama, desegregation campaign in June 1963 when he learned that the chairman of SNCC was stepping down and that he was the favorite to replace him. By this time, Lewis had been arrested twenty-four times. He had demonstrated his commitment to nonviolence and to the movement. At the age of twenty-three, he was a civil rights movement leader. His salary was $10 a week, and SNCC also covered the monthly rent on his Nashville apartment.

As chairman of SNCC, Lewis became a member of the Big Six—the leaders of the six civil rights organizations—the SCLC, SNCC, the National Association for the Advancement of Colored People (NAACP), the National Urban League, CORE, and the Brotherhood of Sleeping Car Porters, the first black labor union. When A. Philip Randolph, head of the Brotherhood, had the idea for a march on Washington, D.C., he called the other five leaders to be partners in the march, whose aim was to pressure President Kennedy to introduce strong civil rights legislation. Lewis, the youngest man in the group by far, made it clear that SNCC would be an equal partner in the planning and implementation of the late August 1963 march. And when it came time for him to give a speech on the steps of the Lincoln Memorial to the crowd of some 250,000 people, he was the most confrontational of the speakers. After Martin Luther King Jr. delivered his "I Have a Dream" speech, Lewis spoke on the theme, "Which side is the federal government on?"

That March, the largest peaceful demonstration in Washington, D.C., to date, was the last peaceful moment of the movement for a long time. The forces of equal rights and the forces of segregation collided again and again over the next two years. Birmingham's Sixteenth Street Baptist Church was bombed in September; President Kennedy was assassinated in Dallas, Texas, in November. SNCC's voter registration campaign in Mississippi in the summer of 1964, for which Lewis was the chief architect, provoked such a backlash that several civil rights workers were killed and hundreds more were beaten and arrested. But in July 1964, President Lyndon B. Johnson signed into law the first strong civil rights legislation since the post–Civil War Reconstruction period.

In the spring of 1965, SNCC launched a voter registration drive in Selma, Alabama. In response, white authorities posted out-to-lunch signs at the courthouse voter registration office. When SNCC organized lines of people to wait as long as was necessary, the sheriff of Selma arrested them for blocking the courthouse entrance. During three days of peaceful protests, more than two hundred people were arrested, including John Lewis (altogether, he was arrested forty times).

A similar protest was taking place in nearby Marion, Alabama, but that protest turned deadly. Police attacked the marchers, and a young black man named Jimmie Lee Jackson was killed trying to protect his mother. Lewis walked with Dr. King at the head of a long line of mourners at the funeral for Jimmie Lee Jackson. Someone suggested that they should keep marching to the state capital of Montgomery, and the idea for the Selma to Montgomery March was born.

The plan had been for Dr. King to lead the march, but after receiving threats on his life, he had decided not to go. His close ally, the Reverend Hosea Williams, would represent the SCLC in his stead. John Lewis would represent SNCC. Late in the afternoon on Sunday, March 7, 1965, Lewis and Williams stood in front of the Brown Chapel African Methodist Episcopal Church in Selma. Behind them were nearly six hundred people, all prepared to set out on the five-day march to the state capital in Montgomery. Lewis had a backpack containing his toothbrush, an apple, and a book. He did not plan to march for the whole five days straight but to give his place to another civil rights leader when it was time for reinforcements to step in.

The marchers headed down Sylvan Street, turned right on Water Street, and then walked to Broad Street. They turned left and headed up the steep western arch of the Edmund Pettus Bridge, which led out of Selma. Several dozen of Selma Sheriff Jim Clark's men watched the marchers as they passed, as did several dozen citizens of Selma. At the crest of the bridge, Lewis suddenly saw a sea of state troopers spread out across the highway on the other side of the bridge. Behind them and on either side were more of Sheriff Clark's men, some on horseback, and what seemed like hundreds of screaming, jeering white people. The commander of the state troopers, Major John Cloud, raised his bullhorn and shouted, "This is an unlawful assembly. . . . You are ordered to disperse and go back to your church or your homes."[2]

Lewis looked back at the frightened marchers. He looked down at the rushing brown waters of the river. He did not know what to do. He could not turn back even if he had wanted to. There were too many black people on the bridge and behind them those crowds of white people with hate in their eyes and voices. Major Cloud's voice boomed through the bullhorn, "You have two minutes to turn around and go back to your church." Lewis turned to Reverend Williams and said, "We should all pray."[3] Williams had been thinking the same thing, and he asked Major Cloud if they could have a moment to pray. There was no answer.

Just as the marchers knelt down to pray—and just one minute after he had issued a two-minute warning—Major Cloud gave the order to attack. Dozens of state troopers swarmed up the bridge span, swinging clubs, those on horseback driving their horses into the crowd. Lewis was hit by a trooper's club. The other marchers tried to turn back, but they were met by Sheriff Clark's men, who attacked them without mercy. Clark's men also attacked the reporters and cameramen who were covering the event, but they were unable to prevent reports and photographs of hundreds of uniformed officers beating defenseless people on what became known as Bloody Sunday.

Lewis was so badly injured that he had to be hospitalized. But as soon as he was able to do so, he rejoined the struggle. On Sunday, March 21, the Selma to Montgomery March began again. This time, many famous celebrities, elected officials, and religious leaders from across the country arrived to show their support of the marchers. President Johnson sent federal troops to protect them. By the time the marchers reached Montgomery, they were twenty-five thousand strong. Five months later, President Johnson signed the Voting Rights Act of 1965, which protected the rights of all Americans to vote. The act made it a crime to use force against anyone trying to register to vote.

By 1966, the civil rights movement had taken on a new, more militant tone. Within SNCC, there were disagreements about how to continue the fight. Many in SNCC no longer wanted to be associated with the SCLC. They wanted to take the fight for equal rights away from the South and to northern cities. Although Lewis won reelection as chairman of SNCC, the election was so highly contested that the rest of the leadership called for another vote. Lewis lost that second vote.

After he was "deelected," as he called it, John Lewis left SNCC. He eventually became director of the Voter Education Project. In 1977, President Jimmy Carter appointed him as head of ACTION, the federal volunteer agency. In 1981, he was elected to the Atlanta City Council, and in 1986, he was elected to Congress as U.S. representative of Georgia's Fifth Congressional District. He has been reelected every two years. Often called "the conscience of the Congress," he was named one of "9 Pillars of Congress" by *Esquire* magazine in November 2006.

PRATHIA HALL WYNN (1940–2002)

Born in Philadelphia, Pennsylvania, the daughter of a Baptist minister, Prathia Lauraann Hall had a comfortable upbringing. She attended predominantly white elementary and high schools and rarely experienced overt racism. But no one who is black in America can escape discrimination completely. When Hall was five, her family traveled south to visit her grandparents. The train conductor was rude to the Halls and forced them to sit in a car behind the engine. In Hall's recollection, that was her first encounter with racism. It was like a stab in the heart, and she remembered it vividly for the rest of her life.

Hall's father, who was pastor of Mount Sharon Baptist Church in north Philadelphia, was a passionate advocate of racial justice. He also believed that each person is a special child of God, particularly his little girl. Hall was tiny when she was first lifted up to stand on a chair to read Scripture. She once said, "I have always been aware of God's presence in my life, and I knew that would have something to do with how I would live my life."[1] She had a fine speaking voice, and her parents trained her, her sisters, and her brother Blakely in elocution. In high school, she was president of the debating society. She won several oratorical contests, which earned her scholarships to attend Temple University.

By the time she was seventeen, the civil rights movement was in progress, and Prathia yearned to be part of it. But she was too young, and her father absolutely forbade it. He died while she was in college, and after that, she felt free to follow her heart. She became a member of the Student Nonviolent Coordinating Committee (SNCC) and undertook Freedom Rides on the Atlantic Seaboard with other college students on the East Coast. SNCC officials soon realized how well spoken she was, so they chose her to speak at fund-raisers and to bring the message of the movement to whoever would listen.

(continued)

PRATHIA HALL WYNN *(continued)*

Hall spent her summers working for the movement. In 1963, she helped write the speech that SNCC chairman John Lewis delivered at the March on Washington. In 1964, she participated in Mississippi Freedom Summer, another SNCC voter registration project. The reaction of Mississippi whites was virulent, and she was beaten and arrested along with many of her fellow workers.

For the first time in her life, Hall began to question the philosophy of nonviolence. She stayed in the movement, however, and in the spring of 1965, she participated in the voter registration drive in Selma, Alabama, which led to the fateful encounter with Alabama state troopers at the Edmund Pettus Bridge in Selma. Much later, thinking back on the strain of not fighting back—not even talking back—she decided, "We might have had even greater power if we had somehow found a way to allow space for the expression of righteous anger."[2]

Hall did not remain in SNCC after more militant forces took over in 1966. She struggled with her crisis of faith for several years before she decided to follow in her father's footsteps and enter the ministry. She became one of the first women ordained in the American Baptist Association and was hired as pastor of the same church over which her father had presided. Hall ministered to her congregation while suffering much personal tragedy. Married to a man named Wynn, she had two children, DuBois Wynn and Simone Denise Wynn. Her daughter suffered a stroke and died at the age of twenty-three, and she herself battled health problems that resulted from a car accident. She died in 2002 from a blood disease.

PART FIVE

✦

LEADERS OF TODAY

V A S H T I   M U R P H Y

McKENZIE

(B . 1 9 4 7)

◆

Today's African American religious leaders have far more opportunities than those who came before them. But they also face barriers. Women religious leaders, for example, still have a much harder time than men. Some say they must be twice as good to get half as far. Reverend Dr. Vashti Murphy McKenzie is among the successful.

She was born Vashti Murphy in Baltimore, Maryland. Her family had deep roots in the Baltimore area and had distinguished themselves in publishing and politics. Her great-grandfather John Murphy had started Baltimore's leading black newspaper, the *Afro-American*, in 1892, and her grandfather and father had continued in the family business. Her grandmother Vashti Turly Murphy, after whom she was named, had been one of the founders of Delta Sigma Theta, the black college sorority.

Vashti's parents were active in St. James Episcopal Church. Vashti attended Sunday school, sang in the youth choir, and attended Bible camp. She had a happy childhood, largely within the comfort of Baltimore's black middle class. Upon graduation from high school, she enrolled in all-black Morgan State University in Baltimore and had her sights set on a career in the family newspaper business. Then she met and fell in love with Stan McKenzie, a guard for the Baltimore Bullets basketball team, who was three years older than she. Vashti was a junior when Stan was traded to the Phoenix Suns. Unwilling to be so far away from the young woman he loved, Stan asked Vashti to marry him and move to Phoenix. Her parents counseled her to wait until she had finished college, but she followed her heart and married Stan. In Phoenix, she worked for a time as a reporter for the *Arizona Republic* and started a family, which would eventually comprise three children: Jon-Michael, Vashti-Jasmine, and Joi-Marie.

As the wife of an NBA basketball player, Vashti McKenzie got used to moving from city to city. After three seasons with the Phoenix Suns, Stan was traded to the brand-new team, the Portland (Oregon) Trail Blazers. After two seasons with Portland, he was traded to the Houston (Texas) Rockets. After two seasons with Houston, he retired in 1973. The McKenzies then moved back to Baltimore, and Vashti, age twenty-seven, resumed her college studies. She graduated from the University of Maryland, College Park, with a degree in journalism.

Vashti went to work for the Murphy family's newspaper, the Baltimore *Afro-American*, and she had her own column, "The McKenzie Report." Seeking a wider audience, she also worked in radio, hosting shows at two local gospel stations. Eventually, she became corporate vice president of programming for WJZ-TV in Baltimore. But her time spent as the host of a radio call-in show eventually inspired a career and life change.

Vashti McKenzie had often been asked by callers for advice about their problems, and she enjoyed helping them. Eventually, she began to question her career choice. She sought counsel from the Reverend John Bryant, the popular minister of Bethel African Methodist Episcopal

(AME) Church in Baltimore. She joined that church, visiting the sick and helping to promote church activities in the media. But she still wanted to do more, and after a period of fasting and praying, she decided to follow the call to the ministry.

McKenzie enrolled at Howard University, the historic black college in Washington, D.C., and received a master of divinity degree. She then earned a doctor of ministry degree from Union Theological Seminary in Dayton, Ohio. She returned to Baltimore and was ordained a deacon in 1984. Her first assignment was as pastor of a seven-member congregation in Chesapeake City, Maryland. After one year there, she was appointed pastor of Oak Street AME Church in Baltimore. A few years later, she became the first woman pastor in the hundred-plus-year history of Payne Memorial AME Church, in Baltimore's inner city.

It was at Payne that the Reverend Dr. McKenzie fully put into practice her belief that the church could make a difference not only in the spiritual lives but also in the day-to-day lives of her parishioners. With the support of her congregation, she developed the Human Economic Development Center to provide job training and placement, programs for senior citizens, and youth and adult education programs. She also helped organize a group of churches and banks into the Collective Banking Group to ensure equal opportunity for the black residents of Baltimore. With each new effort, her congregation increased, growing from fewer than four hundred fifty when she arrived to over fifteen hundred.

During her career as a clergywoman, Dr. McKenzie often came up against the "stained-glass ceiling," by which she meant the barriers to the advancement of women in the church. In 1995, she decided to break through that stained-glass ceiling by seeking the office of bishop. In the 213-year history of the AME Church, there had never been a woman bishop. Vashti McKenzie was determined to become the first. She campaigned for that position in the same way as a politician campaigns for election to public office. She used her media experience to promote her candidacy. In 2000, she became the first woman bishop in the AME Church.

JESSE L. JACKSON (B. 1941)

Jesse Jackson was born in Greenville, North Carolina. His mother, Helen Burns, was unmarried, and young Jesse was taunted by his classmates for having "no daddy." When he was two, his mother married Charles Jackson, who tried hard to make Jesse feel as if he belonged. By the time he was ten years old, Jesse realized there was another way he did not belong: he was not white and thus did not belong with white people—at least not in segregated Greensboro. Despite these strikes against him, Jesse Jackson grew up to be a popular, athletic young man who won a football scholarship to the University of Illinois in 1959. He was surprised and hurt when he got there and discovered that African Americans were not allowed to play quarterback.

The following year, students at North Carolina Agricultural and Technical College, a black college in Greensboro, North Carolina, began to protest the segregation laws by sitting in at the lunch counter of the local Woolworth's and refusing to leave until they were served. After several months, during which the black students were joined by students from local white colleges, Woolworth's gave in, opening the lunch counter to all who wished to eat there.

Jesse Jackson was electrified; revolutionary things were happening in his home state, and he wanted to be part of them. He transferred to North Carolina A&T, where he became the star quarterback on the football team and a leader in student government. He involved himself in civil rights work and joined the Southern Christian Leadership Conference (SCLC). He also became a husband, marrying fellow student Jacqueline Brown when he was a sophomore and she was a freshman. He graduated in 1964 with a degree in sociology.

Religion had always been part of Jackson's life, but it was his work with the civil rights movement that pointed him toward the ministry as a career. He attended workshops led by Dr. Martin Luther King Jr. and realized that he could do much to change conditions for his people as a minister. After his graduation from college, Jesse and Jacqueline Jackson headed north to Chicago, where Jesse enrolled at Chicago Theological Seminary. But he soon left to return to the South to work with Dr. King and the SCLC.

(continued)

JESSE L. JACKSON *(continued)*

The SCLC had formed Operation Breadbasket to mount boycotts to force businesses to employ more African Americans, and Jackson was named national director in 1967. He grew close to Dr. King and was with the SCLC leader in Memphis, Tennessee, in 1968 when King was assassinated. In the aftermath of the King assassination, Jackson's relationships with the SCLC became strained. He left the organization, forming his own, Operation PUSH (People United to Save Humanity), in 1971.

In 1983, Jackson carried his message of empowerment to a broader audience of poor and dispossessed people of all races, forming the Rainbow Coalition. He campaigned for the 1984 Democratic presidential nomination, and although he did not win it, he made a respectable showing in several primary elections. He was very successful in promoting voter registration. He ran again for the Democratic presidential nomination in 1988 and won nearly seven million votes.

Although Jackson himself never achieved elected office, his son, Jesse Jr., was elected to Congress from Chicago in 1995 and has been reelected every two years since then.

Jesse Jackson Sr. has achieved national stature. He served as an adviser to President Bill Clinton during Clinton's eight years in office, 1992–2000, and in 2000 he was awarded the nation's highest civilian honor, the Presidential Medal of Freedom. Jackson has used his influence to press a variety of civil and human rights causes, including the end of apartheid in South Africa, statehood for the District of Columbia, and a society free of illegal drugs. He regards the world as his platform and thus in 2005 he agreed to help with Great Britain's Operation Black Vote, a campaign to encourage more of England's ethnic minorities to vote in political elections. In 2007, he undertook a tour of Great Britain's inner cities to campaign against guns and illegal drugs. He has made the campaign against guns a special cause and in June 2007 was arrested outside a gun store in a poor neighborhood in Chicago. As the most famous African American leader, Jackson is often regarded as a representative of all black Americans. He uses his influence for good wherever and whenever he can.

She was sent to Southeast Africa, where she served as chief pastor of the Eighteenth Episcopal District. Based in the Kingdom of Lesotho, a tiny landlocked country surrounded by South Africa, she developed programs to increase education and employment and to assist those suffering from AIDS. She currently serves as the presiding prelate of the Thirteenth Episcopal District, encompassing Tennessee and Kentucky.

Dr. McKenzie considers herself a "womanist." "Womanism" is an African American version of feminism. She has written two books, *Not Without Struggle* (1996) and *Strength in the Struggle* (2000), and has crafted the Ten Commandments for African American Clergywomen and the Ten Womanist Commandments for Clergy.

FREDERICK J.
STREETS

(B. 1950)

✦

Today's African American religious leaders have made remarkable strides at the top American universities. Among them is the Reverend Dr. Peter J. Gomes, who became chaplain of Harvard University's Memorial Chapel in 1970. By the early twenty-first century, five of the eight Ivy League schools had black university chaplains. Frederick J. Streets was appointed chaplain of Yale University and senior pastor of the Church of Christ at Yale in 1992.

Streets, who is known as Jerry to his friends, was born of mixed parentage. His father was African American and his mother was an Afro-Polish American. He was raised to identify with African Americans by color but also to appreciate the Polish traditions of his maternal grandmother. He was taught that being a spiritual, moral, and ethical person was more important than being black or white or both.

Streets grew up on the South Side of Chicago. His parents were active in the Antioch Missionary Baptist Church, and Streets grew up feeling comfortable in the church and finding a sense of community there. He was drawn to Antioch's pastor, the Reverend W. N. Daniel. In fact, by the age of fourteen, he had decided to follow in the Reverend Daniel's footsteps and become a minister himself. He wore an Austin Powers–like suit, but without the frills, and kept a Bible under his arm. He told people that he was going to be the first teenage Billy Graham, referring to the first television preacher. People began calling him "Preacher Streets."

He became interested in how people make connections and find community. At Ottawa University in Kansas, he majored in psychology and also took as many courses as he could in racial and ethnic history. Streets even did independent research at the Institute on Race Relations in London. The more he learned, the more he understood that different groups of people have much in common.

Streets graduated from the University of Ottawa with a bachelor's degree in psychology and sociology in 1972. He then enrolled at Yale Divinity School in New Haven. Traditionally, there was not much communication between Yale and its surrounding community, but that was not Frederick J. Streets's way. While a student at Yale, he served on the New Haven Board of Aldermen, which is the local government. Also while at Yale, Streets got married. He and his wife have one daughter, Carolyn.

Streets graduated from Yale Divinity School in the spring of 1975. By December, he had a job as pastor of Mount Aery Baptist Church in Bridgeport, Connecticut. Named for Mount Ararat in the Bible, the place where Noah's Ark was supposed to have come to rest after the great flood, Mount Aery had been founded in 1923 in the home of Mrs. Simon Woods. By 1975, it had outgrown the building on Wallace Street that the congregation had purchased in 1938. The Reverend Streets became pastor after his predecessor passed away. He was only the fourth pastor in the history of the church, but he became the most activist.

The bespectacled new pastor was open-faced, friendly, and burning with energy. He based his philosophy of pastoral care on the work of his own pastor in Chicago, the Reverend W. N. Daniel of the Antioch Missionary Baptist Church. He also credited the influence of Dr. Martin Luther King Jr., Dr. Edwin Edmonds, the pastor of the historic Dixwell Avenue United Church of Christ in New Haven, Connecticut, and the Reverend Howard Thurman. He admired the Church of All People in San Francisco, the integrated, multicultural churches that Thurman had founded.

One of the first things the Reverend Streets did was to launch a building fund. It took six years, but the congregation raised enough money to purchase property from an electronics factory on Frank Street. The Reverend Streets then secured commitments from seven banks to lend the congregation the money needed to build a new church, which was dedicated in 1982. The most arresting part of the church is an eighty-five-foot-high cross weighing seven tons that rises from the church lobby. It can be seen for miles around.

Next, the Reverend Streets turned his attention more fully to the day-to-day needs of his congregation. Over the next dozen years, he introduced outreach programs for the elderly, scholarships for young people, and programs to distribute food to the hungry. He created an AIDS ministry, an after-school program, and a health and social service education and referral service. Most of these programs were fairly typical of urban ministries. But the Reverend Streets went further. He created a church-sponsored development corporation to build affordable housing.

Meanwhile, he continued to advance his education in order to help his people. He earned a master's degree in social work and a doctorate in social welfare from the Wurzweiler School of Social Work at Yeshiva University in New York. He also earned certificates from Harvard University's Program on Professional Education and the Staff College of the National Institutes of Mental Health. Streets served as a psychiatric social work associate at the Greater Bridgeport Community Mental Health Center and the Child Guidance Center of Bridgeport, and as a research associate and a teacher at Hartford Seminary. He also served as an adjunct professor of pastoral theology at Yale Divinity School in nearby New Haven. By the early 1990s, he was nationally known as a smart, hardworking, dedicated religious and community leader. Still, it was headline news when Yale University tapped him for the position of university chaplain.

Appointed in 1992, the Reverend Streets was the first African American and the first Baptist minister to serve in this position. The Yale University chaplain serves as senior pastor of the Church of Christ at Yale, which was founded in 1757. The chaplain also officiates at functions such as commencement services and works with the leaders of at least a dozen denominational ministries at the school—different Christian faiths as well as Muslim, Jewish, and Baha'i. The Yale chaplaincy has roots in the eighteenth century and has always been filled by a minister from a more traditional Protestant church, such as the Congregationalist Church or the Church of Christ. The Church of Christ at Yale had come a long way from its Puritan past. In fact, in 1989, it had added an open and affirming statement to its mission, a testament to its determination to embrace diversity.

Nevertheless, in his first years as chaplain at Yale, Streets came up against prejudice and stereotyping not only because he was black but also because he was Baptist. One of the white members of his church informed him that the only blacks he had known previously were servants. Others worried that he would be straitlaced and rigid, associating him with the Southern Baptist Church, to which he did not belong.

But these were minor obstacles. For an activist minister and a student of human history and human nature such as the Reverend Streets, the Yale chaplaincy was an ideal position. He remained on the faculty of Yale Divinity School and also joined the clinical social faculty of the Yale Child Study Center, giving him the opportunity to pursue many interests.

While at Yale, Streets had many opportunities to travel. He visited Bosnia as a senior consultant with the Harvard University Program in

Refugee Trauma and was part of delegations to Cuba, Colombia, and Argentina. In 2000, he was a delegate to the first world conference of religious leaders to convene at the United Nations. Ever more engaged in world issues, he left Yale University after fifteen years, in July 2007, to accept a faculty position at Wurzweiler School of Social Work at Yeshiva University in New York, where he had earned his graduate degrees. In the spring of 2008 he will take a leave from that post to spend a semester at the University of Pretoria in South Africa where as a Fulbright Scholar he will study families with children suffering from HIV and AIDS and the ways medical and social work can support the spirituality of those families.

The Reverend Streets published a book, *Preaching in the New Millennium* (Yale University Press, 2005). It is devoted to the theme to which he has devoted his life's work: the creation of community. Here are some of his thoughts on that subject:

> Studying about racial and ethnic history should be encouraged. Learning this history will show connections, not differences, and is important to the future of democracy. The quality of our sense of community is related to freedom. Freedom is related to how we treat each other.[1]

A L
SHARPTON

(B . 1 9 5 4)

✦

The Reverend Al Sharpton's approach to the fight for racial justice often harkens back to the days of the direct-action civil rights movement. Born one year before Rosa Parks refused to give up her seat on a Montgomery, Alabama, bus to a white man, which led to her arrest and sparked the Montgomery Bus Boycott, Sharpton was influenced by some of the younger leaders of the movement. But he is a minister in the Pentecostal Church, whereas the others were Baptist ministers. And unlike most of the leaders of the civil rights movement, he has waged his campaign for justice in the North, usually in Brooklyn, New York.

"I was always a preacher," writes Sharpton in his autobiography, *Go and Tell the Pharoah*.[1] He started preaching in public when he was four years old. He delivered the sermon for the anniversary service of his church, Washington Temple Church of God in Christ, in Brooklyn. It was a Pentecostal church, part of the movement in Evangelical Christianity that emphasizes the personal experience of religious conversion through baptism. Evangelicals believe that the Bible is literally true, that salvation can only come through faith in Jesus Christ, that all Christians should be publicly baptized as a confession of faith, and that they must evangelize, or spread the faith.

That first time he preached, as a four-year-old, little Alfred Sharpton had to stand on a box to be seen above the pulpit. But he was so passionate that Bishop Frederick Douglass Washington, pastor of the church, allowed him to preach the sermon once a month. By the time Sharpton was in first grade, he was writing his name as Reverend Alfred Sharpton.

Washington Temple Church of God in Christ was like a second home to young Sharpton. It occupied a former movie theater that took up an entire block, and it was overflowing with worshippers at every service. Bishop Washington was a down-home type of preacher who could whoop and holler but who was also a learned man. From him, Al Sharpton learned that the successful black preacher is a combination religious leader, social leader, social worker, and entertainer. Referring to the black church as an institution, Sharpton later wrote, "I now see that it was the only place that black people of that generation could be somebody."[2]

The Sharptons led a comfortable life. Alfred Charles Sharpton Sr. owned a store and put every penny of money he could save into buying apartment buildings. Ada Richards Sharpton had supported herself as a seamstress before her marriage; afterward, she stayed home to keep house and take care of her children. She had a daughter by a former marriage, and another daughter and Alfred Jr. with Alfred Sharpton Sr. But everything changed when Al Jr. was about ten and his parents divorced. His father moved out of the house, his mother suffered a nervous breakdown, and after she recovered, she moved herself and her children into a housing project in Brooklyn.

Not long after his parents were divorced, young Al Sharpton was ordained and licensed as a Pentecostal minister. Bishop Washington named him junior minister. He preached on Friday nights for free, as part of his service to the church, but on Sundays he got to keep the money that was taken up during the collection. Boy preachers were not uncommon in the Pentecostal Church, but young Al Sharpton was special. He was in great demand not only in Brooklyn but elsewhere in New York City and far beyond. He traveled with the great gospel singers Mahalia Jackson and Roberta Martin, preaching all over the country and the Caribbean. With such worldly experience, it was hard for him to be a normal boy. His worry about his mother's illness and his father's departure caused him to lose concentration. He might have gotten into trouble if he had not been taken under the wing of some of his teachers.

Al was eleven years old when he bought a book about Adam Clayton Powell Jr. and was inspired by the older man's story, deciding that he, too, wanted to have not just a religious ministry but also a political and social one. One Sunday, he and his sister took the subway to Harlem, to Powell's Abyssinian Baptist Church. After the service, Al spent the afternoon with Powell, witnessing the incredible power that the older man had and the adoration he enjoyed from the ordinary people of Harlem.

Al also admired Dr. Martin Luther King Jr. and was devastated by his assassination. Al joined Operation Breadbasket, an organization that had been founded by the Southern Christian Leadership Conference (SCLC) to boycott corporations and picket places of business with the goal of improving job opportunities and economic life for black people. Through Operation Breadbasket, he came to know the Reverend Jesse Jackson, who had joined the SCLC and been a top aide to Dr. Martin Luther King Jr. After King's death, Jackson and the Reverend Ralph David Abernathy, another King aide, had been unable to agree on the future direction of the SCLC, and Jackson had left the organization. He formed his own organization in Chicago, Operation PUSH (People United to Save Humanity). Sharpton applauded Jackson's move.

By 1969, Sharpton was youth director of Operation Breadbasket in Brooklyn. He was a fine organizer, able to persuade people to join picket lines and boycott clothing stores. But he was frustrated that the sort of mass movement that had occurred in the South could not be repeated. Even in Chicago, the Reverend Jesse Jackson had managed to mobilize a good proportion of the city's black population through his economic improvement organization, Operation PUSH. But New York was different. There were pockets of black settlement, but black people lived in many neighborhoods. It was hard to get them together. And Sharpton believed that the media, a huge power in New York, deliberately ignored the pickets and boycotts in one neighborhood so that people in other neighborhoods would not find out about them. As he put it, "The Civil Rights Movement never came to New York."[3]

That did not stop him from trying to create one, however. He formed the National Youth Movement, which he saw as a young people's version of Operation Breadbasket. He organized demonstrations against major corporations and hospitals to demand more hiring of black employees and more advertising in black magazines and newspapers. He began to hold a weekly rally to show strength in numbers.

Sharpton graduated from high school in 1972 and enrolled in Brooklyn College. But he did not remain there. He was too busy being an activist, traveling around the country starting National Youth Movement chapters. One of the biggest regrets of his life is that he did not get his degree. After he met the legendary soul singer James Brown, Sharpton concentrated the efforts of the National Youth Movement on the music business, which had long exploited black singers, musicians, and composers. He organized pickets and boycotts to encourage the hiring of black accountants, managers, and promoters. In the meantime, he kept up an ambitious schedule of preaching and had a circuit of black churches where he gave regular sermons.

Beginning in the 1980s, Sharpton was often the leader of protests against white racial violence and police brutality in the New York black community. When a black man was chased into oncoming traffic by a mob of whites, struck by a car, and killed in the Queens neighborhood of Howard Beach, Sharpton organized protests against that racial murder. Soon, "Howard Beach!" became a rallying cry against racism. In this way, he made the transition from leading young people to leading adults.

Most famous was the case of Tawana Brawley, who charged that she had been sexually assaulted by white men, including police officers, near her home in upstate New York. Although the local authorities had investigated the case, they had not been able to find any suspects. Sharpton led the campaign to bring attention back to the case, charging that the authorities would have worked harder if Brawley had been white. In the end, however, Brawley's story proved to be untrue and the entire case a hoax, which was an embarrassment for Sharpton and a setback for his cause. But there would be many more cases of racial murder and violence that were not hoaxes. The Reverend Al Sharpton became a familiar presence on the local news in New York City, championing the cause of powerless black families whose loved ones had been murdered or beaten or falsely arrested by the police or by racist whites.

In 1992, Sharpton ran for a New York seat in the U.S. Senate. His mentor, Jesse Jackson, had run a respectable campaign for president in 1984 and 1988, and Sharpton felt that those campaigns had done a lot to bring issues of racial injustice to national attention. He decided to do the same through a campaign of his own, also feeling it would be a good way to encourage people to register and vote. He ran a serious campaign, taking positions that were well researched and thought out. Because Sharpton's campaign did not raise a lot of money, he could not buy ad spots on television and radio. Nevertheless, on primary election day, he received over two-thirds of the black vote and bested the much better financed campaign of Elizabeth Holtzman, a former congresswoman and Brooklyn district attorney. But New York State Attorney General Robert Abrams won the primary, although in the November general election he lost to Republican Senator Alfonse D'Amato.

The following year, Sharpton was jailed. His imprisonment stemmed from a rally he had led to protest the Howard Beach murder. Arrested for failing to obtain a permit for the rally, he had been convicted and sentenced to forty-five days in jail. After appeals were unsuccessful, he went to jail in 1993. Thirty days later, an aide to the mayor arranged for him to have work release to his own office. It was not the first time Sharpton had served time in jail. In fact, to that point, he had been arrested twenty times and jailed five times, though only for five days each time. He did not mind going to jail for a short time. As Martin Luther King Jr. had demonstrated, it dramatized political cases that might otherwise go unnoticed. It was Sharpton's mission to, as he wrote, "create theater and drama of an intensity in New York City that people around the rest of the country would say, 'I thought New York was a liberal place, why are they throwing those bricks? Why are those black ministers going to jail? . . . What's going on?'"[4]

Sharpton again ran for the Senate in 1994 and won a larger vote total—87 percent of the black vote. In 1997, he ran for mayor of New York City. But his major emphasis has been the mobilization of black New Yorkers to protest racial violence and murder. When unarmed West African immigrant Amadou Diallo was killed in a hail of police bullets, it was Al Sharpton to whom the Diallo family turned. He served as spokesman for the family in demanding a full investigation of the event and damages paid to the family.

Although he is accused by his critics of being a professional trouble-maker, Sharpton has become a celebrity, with his own radio show, three published books, and a growing public respect for never wavering in his cause. "Everything I've tried to do has been a Christian walk," he wrote in his autobiography, "an effort to live the gospel, to live the sermons I preached when I was young, to feed the hungry, shelter the homeless, comfort the afflicted."[5]

RENITA J.
WEEMS

(B. 1954)

✦

Like the Reverend Vashti Murphy McKenzie, the Reverend Renita J. Weems is a womanist. She studies the Scriptures looking for lessons that are applicable to women today and is especially interested in the lives of women in the Bible. She chose the vocations of teaching and writing over the option of pastoring a church. She prefers to conduct her ministry through her teachings and writings.

The Reverend Weems was born in Atlanta, Georgia, and raised as a Pentecostal. In this atmosphere of passionate embrace of a personal God, where the presence of the Word was communicated by bodily possession and speaking in tongues, young Renita Weems was curiously unmoved. She was by nature analytical and more interested in the life of the mind. She was seventeen years old when she was called to the front of the church and told that God was going to use her to do great works for Him. As she recalled years later, she knew she was supposed to fall on the floor in awe of God's prophetic power. But she did no such thing. Instead, she listened very carefully to what the preacher said to her. When he was finished, she returned to her seat knowing that she had not responded as expected. It was an interesting event but not life-changing.

What bothered Renita most about Pentecostalism was the sense of self-righteousness that people in the church seemed to possess. As a child, she would go around saying things like, "The Lord told me . . ." or "The Lord showed me . . ." But she began to feel that people used God to rationalize their own choices, both the good and the bad—their intention to have their way, their fear of making a decision. At length, she decided to stop blaming God. As she later wrote, she swore off saying such things "until I was prepared to die for my convictions that I'd heard God correctly."[1] She characterizes herself as a "recovering Pentecostal."

Renita Weems came of age when there were many more opportunities for black people, and for black women, than in the past. She attended Wellesley College in Massachusetts and decided on a career in finance. She went to work for the accounting firm of Coopers & Lybrand in Boston and later worked as a stockbroker for Merrill Lynch in New York. But she felt that something was missing in her life.

"I'm one of those who graduated from college and then discovered that I like the world of books and reading and the academic world—the world of the mind. I wanted to be a poet and a novelist more than anything else."[2] Although Weems enrolled in divinity school, she was more interested in writing a novel than in a religious life. In fact, she chose Princeton Theological Seminary because it was close to New York City, where she hoped to find an audience for her poetry and publishing contacts for the novel she planned to write. But in time, her interest in religion took over, and she never did write that novel.

At Princeton Seminary, Weems became deeply interested in the study of the Bible. She was also drawn to women's studies. She found herself applying feminist or womanist theory to her religious studies. She earned both her master's degree and her doctorate at Princeton. She is the first black woman to have received the Ph.D. in Old Testament (1989). While still a doctoral candidate at the seminary, Weems made a speech in San Diego. Afterward, she was approached by a publisher who was looking for African American women who wrote on matters of spirituality. Weems had certainly thought of writing a book, although her plan was to write a novel.

After that chance meeting, she began to look at her speeches and study lessons and to imagine them taking shape as a nonfiction book. Her first book was a direct result of that chance meeting. *Just a Sister Away: A Womanist Vision of Women's Relationships in the Bible* was published in 1991. In its preface, she stated outright that she was writing for African American women "because I thought there were too few books written for them." That book was followed two years later by another, *I Asked for Intimacy: Stories of Blessings, Betrayals and Birthings.*

Although she was ordained in the African Methodist Episcopal Church in 1984 when she was thirty years old, the Reverend Weems did not seek a position as pastor of a church. Instead, she took a job teaching Old Testament studies at the divinity school of Vanderbilt University in Nashville, Tennessee, where she met the Reverend Martin L. Espinosa, founder and senior pastor of the Ray of Hope Community Church. They married and had one daughter, Savannah Nia Weems Espinosa.

The writings and speeches of the Reverend Dr. Weems earned her the recognition of *Ebony* magazine, which in 1998 named her the fourth best black female preacher in the nation. The Reverend Jeremiah A. Wright said in the magazine article that Weems "combines the scholarship of a Ph.D. in Old Testament and Hebrew languages with the Deep South's wisdom of Black women who have known hard times." Ahead of her on the *Ebony* list were the Reverends Prathia Hall, Carolyn Knight, and Vashti Murphy McKenzie. Since only about a third of the Reverend Weems's time was devoted to preaching, as opposed to teaching, writing, and delivering speeches, that was a great honor indeed.

Although her life was full and happy, even the Reverend Weems experienced times when her faith seemed to desert her. One of those times was in the late 1990s. She felt as if God were absent from her life and found her faith wavering. She came to understand, however, that just because she could not hear God, it did not mean that He was not with her. She also learned not to think too much, not to try to apply logic to a faith that transcends logic. She recounted her struggles in *Listening for God: A Minister's Journey Through Silence and Doubt*, published in 1999. Her honesty in communicating her own doubts endeared her to readers and gave them hope that they could triumph in their own spiritual struggles.

At this writing, the Reverend Weems's list of published books includes *Showing Mary: How Women Can Share Prayers, Wisdom, and the Blessings of God* (2002); *Battered Love: Marriage, Sex, and Violence in the Hebrew Prophets*, based on her Princeton Seminary doctoral dissertation (2003); *What Matters Most: Ten Lessons in Living Passionately from the Song of Solomon* (2004); and *Just a Sister Away: Understanding the Timeless Connection Between Women of Today and Women in the Bible* (2005). She also contributes a bimonthly column for the online publication www.beliefnet.com.

While writing books and columns, Weems continued to teach. In the 2003–2004 academic year, she took a leave from Vanderbilt University to serve as the 2003 Cosby Professor at Spelman College in her native Atlanta. The position, funded by the comedian Bill Cosby and his wife, Camille, brings nationally known scholars to the historically black women's college for one year.

The Reverend Weems's latest effort is a consulting firm named "Something Within," advertised as being "for thinking women of faith about matters of church, race, gender, sex, values, culture, justice, spirituality, and, oh yeah, God." She maintains a daily blog at somethingwithin~rjweems.blogspot.com and invites visitors to share their own thoughts on the blog.

T. D.
JAKES

(B . 1 9 5 7)

✦

T. D. Jakes is a Pentecostal minister, raised in the same tradition as the Reverend Renita Weems and the Reverend Al Sharpton. But Jakes is a neo-Pentecostalist. Also called the charismatic movement, this branch of the Christian faith has an enthusiastic approach to religious practice that includes baptism of the Holy Spirit and belief in the gifts of the Spirit, such as speaking in tongues, healing, and prophecy. Rather than being an independent church, it remains within the established Protestant—and also Catholic—churches and seeks to integrate Spirit baptism and gifts into the practices of those churches. In its early days, Pentecostalism meant choosing a life of simplicity and not worrying about the accumulation of material possessions. Nowadays, the gospel of prosperity is right at home in the Pentecostal Church. No Pentecostal minister is more prosperous than the Reverend T. D. Jakes.

Thomas Dexter Jakes was born in Charleston, West Virginia, in Vandalia Hill, a neighborhood that overlooks the city. As a boy, Jakes had the nickname "Tommy from the Hill." He later acquired the nickname "Bible Boy" for his habit of carrying the Bible around with him wherever he went.

His parents were not especially religious. His father was a Methodist, his mother a Baptist who sometimes attended First Baptist Church of Vandalia. Young Tommy Jakes responded to the sense of community the church provided more than his mother did and became active in the choir. He was talented musically, and his mother bought him a piano when he was an adolescent.

Vandalia Hill was racially mixed, and Jakes did not encounter racism as a child. His major problem was being overweight. He got that from his father, who weighed three hundred pounds. But he also realized early on that his family was poor and could not afford to buy him a Snoopy lunch box, instead sending him to school with a greasy brown lunch bag.

His father, Ernest, worked as a janitor at a local grocery store and at the West Virginia capitol building. On the side, he sold whatever he could get from the back of his truck, including fish and frog legs. His mother, Odith, taught grade school and sold Avon products in her spare time. She also kept a garden, and by the time he was eight, Tommy Jakes was selling her vegetables. By the time he was ten, he was also selling Avon products.

After Ernest Jakes was diagnosed with a kidney disease, he was forced to stop working. The family income plunged, and so did the family stability. Jakes's parents separated and then divorced. His father died when Jakes was fifteen years old.

Jakes turned to religion for solace. One night, he accompanied the First Baptist Church of Vandalia choir to a small Pentecostal church called Greater Emmanuel Gospel Tabernacle. The service emphasized the presence of the Holy Spirit. Tommy Jakes cried out, "Lord, if it is real then let it happen to me."[1] Immediately, he began speaking in tongues, evidence of the experience of God's power. He left First Baptist Church and joined Greater Emmanuel Gospel Tabernacle, but he had a difficult time there, surrounded by people who were so self-righteous that he didn't feel he could ever measure up. Years later, he said that the experience cured him of ever feeling he was "holier" than the next person.

Struggling with depression, Jakes dropped out of school and went to work as part-time musical director at his former church. Later, he finished his high school equivalency requirements. He enrolled at West Virginia State College, majoring in psychology, but found that he could not handle his college work on top of his job at a local chemical plant. He was called to the ministry when he was seventeen years old and added preaching in area storefront churches to his schedule of activities. He started his own ten-member church in the coal-mining town of Montgomery in 1979, where he met and married a young woman named Serita, who also suffered from weight problems and low self-esteem.

In 1982, a year after his marriage, Jakes began broadcasting his sermons over a local radio station. In 1985, he moved his church to the larger town of Smithers, taking over an old movie theater. Five years later, he moved his growing congregation to South Charleston. After the congregation doubled, he moved the church again, this time to a predominantly white suburb called Cross Lanes.

Jakes had occasional invitations to preach in other states, and it was a big step forward for him when Bishop Ernestine Reems, founder and pastor of a Pentecostal church named Hope Community Church in Oakland, California, invited him to speak at her church. She encouraged him to continue pursuing his dreams of having his own huge, nationally known church. But his big break came when he met Sarah Jordan Powell, a well-known gospel singer, who invited him to attend the 1992 Azusa Conference in Tulsa, Oklahoma.

The Pentecostal revival of the early twentieth century began with a 1906 religious conference on Azusa Street in San Francisco, California. The Azusa conferences in the 1990s were attempts to capture the fervor and power of that earlier revival. At the 1992 conference, Sarah Powell introduced Jakes to Carlton Pearson, a noted television evangelist who was the adopted son of the white evangelist Oral Roberts. Some months later, Pearson invited Jakes to preach at a regional meeting of ministers. Jakes's hour-long sermon, "Behind Closed Doors," was a great success. In fact, the owner of a Christian broadcasting network played the tape every Friday night for eight weeks, giving Jakes his first national exposure.

Jakes was invited to preach at the Azusa Conference the following year. Six-foot-three, weighing three hundred pounds, and dressed in his best suit, which was shiny from too much washing and pressing, he won over the crowd with his sermon, "Woman, Thou Art Loosed." He harked back to his early days in the Greater Emmanuel Gospel Tabernacle, when he was depressed and feeling unworthy among self-righteous people. He said it was a terrible thing to be in trouble when you are in church; when you are in church, you are not supposed to be in trouble. He intoned, "Spirit of the living God, breathe in this place. Release an anointing because somebody in this room is in trouble. Somebody's wife is in trouble, some mother of the church, some first lady is in trouble; encumbered with duties and responsibilities. Functioning like a robot but bleeding like a wounded dog."[2]

It was as if he had put his finger on the pain of the audience, most of whom were women. They were crying and screaming and jumping up and down. They rushed to buy the tape of his sermon. Pastors from all over the country wanted to book him as guest preacher. The same owner of the broadcasting network that had carried his previous year's sermon offered to broadcast all of his sermons. He was an overnight success.

T. D. Jakes rose to fame in an unprecedented amount of time. Videotapes and television can reach millions and breed megastars. He published a book of the same title as his famous sermon and quickly followed it with four other books, started his own television show, *Get Ready with T. D. Jakes*, and launched a nationally syndicated radio version of his television broadcast. Membership in Temple of Faith, his own church in Charleston, West Virginia, jumped to nearly one thousand parishioners.

He was rich, and he and Sarita lived a luxurious lifestyle, with expensive clothes and cars and a mansion with an indoor bowling alley and a swimming pool. In 1996, he relocated to Dallas, Texas, and established a new church called "Potter's House" in a five-thousand-seat building that had formerly housed the church of another evangelist preacher. Almost two thousand people joined the church on its opening Sunday. Three years later, having outgrown the space, Potter's House broke ground for a new, eight-thousand-seat church. By the time that building was ready, membership had grown to nearly twenty-four thousand.

In 2001, *Time* magazine featured T. D. Jakes on its cover and listed him among the twenty-five most influential evangelicals in America. By that time, he had published more nonfiction books and a novel, started a production company, and had a personal fortune estimated at more than $100 million. He had combined his postmodern brand of spirituality with the business sense of a twenty-first–century tycoon.

NOTES

ABSALOM JONES AND RICHARD ALLEN

1. James Henretta, "Richard Allen and African-American Identity: A Black Ex-Slave in Early America's White Society Preserves His Cultural Identity by Creating Separate Institutions," *The Early America Review*. Available online at http://www.earlyamerica.com/review/.

LEMUEL HAYNES

1. *Africans in America*. Part II. Lemuel Haynes. WGBH. PBS Online.

JOHN MARRANT

1. Joanna Brooks. "*John Marrant's Journal*: Providence and Prophecy in the Eighteenth-Century Black Atlantic." *North Star*, Vol. 3, No. 1 (Fall 1999).

SOJOURNER TRUTH

1. Sojourner Truth, Olive Gilbert, and Frances W. Titus, *Narrative of Sojourner Truth; a Bondswoman of Olden Time, Emancipated by the New York Legislature in the Early Part of the Present Century; with a History of Her Labors and Correspondence, Drawn from Her "Book of Life."* Boston: For the Author, 1875, p. 17. Electronic Edition: Documenting the American South, University of North Carolina, Chapel Hill. http://docsouth.unc.edu/neh/truth75/menu.html.

2. Ibid., p. 27.

3. Ibid., p. 109.

NAT TURNER

1. Thomas R. Gray, *The Confessions of Nat Turner, The Leader of the Late Insurrection in South Hampton, Va.* Baltimore, MD, 1831, p. 7. Electronic edition: Documenting the American South, University of North Carolina, Chapel Hill. http://docsouth.unc.edu/neh/turner/menu.html.

2. Ibid., p. 9.

3. Ibid., p. 13.

4. William Wells Brown, *The Black Man, His Antecedents, His Genius, and His Achievements.* New York: Thomas Hamilton, 48 Beekman Street, 1863, p. 63. Electronic edition: Documenting the American South, University of North Carolina, Chapel Hill. http://docsouth.unc.edu/brownww/brown.html#brown59.

5. Ibid.

6. Gray, p. 19.

7. Brown, p. 65.

MARIA STEWART

1. Women's History Resources at the American Antiquarian Society. http://www.americanantiquarian.org/womensstudies.htm.

JOHN JASPER

1. William E. Hatcher, *John Jasper: The Unmatched Negro Philosopher and Preacher.* New York: Fleming H. Revell Company, 1908, p. 75. Electronic edition: Documenting the American South, University of North Carolina, http://docsouth.unc.edu/church/hatcher/menu.html.

2. Ibid., p. 59.

3. Edwin Archer Randolph, *The Life of Rev. John Jasper, Pastor of Sixth Mt. Zion Baptist Church, Richmond, Va., from His Birth to the Present Time, with His Theory on the Rotation of the Sun.* Richmond, VA: R. T. Hill & Co., Publishers, 1884. Electronic edition: Documenting the American South, University of North Carolina, http://docsouth.unc.edu/church/hatcher/menu.html.

4. Hatcher, p. 95.

5. Ibid., p. 129.

ALEXANDER CRUMMELL

1. Walter L. Williams, *Black Americans and the Evangelization of Africa, 1877–1900.* Madison: University of Wisconsin Press, 1982, p. 11.

2. Ibid., p. 11.

HENRY MCNEAL TURNER

1. William J. Simmons, *Men of Mark: Eminent, Progressive and Rising,* reprint edition. Chicago: Johnson Publishing Co., 1970, p. 810.

2. Ibid., p. 814.

3. Ibid., p. 817.

VERNON JOHNS

1. Patrick L. Cooney and Henry W. Powell, *The Life and Times of the Prophet Vernon Johns: Father of the Civil Rights Movement.* Farmville, VA: The Vernon Johns Society, 1998.

LOUIS FARRAKHAN

1. Claude Andrew Clegg III, *An Original Man: The Life and Times of Elijah Muhammad.* New York: St. Martin's Press, 1998, p. 156.

HOWARD THURMAN

1. Howard Thurman, *With Head and Heart: The Autobiography of Howard Thurman.* New York: Harcourt, Brace, Jovanovich, 1979.

2. Ibid., p. 36.

3. Ibid., p. 45.

4. Jean Burden, *"Howard Thurman," Chicken Bones: A Journal for Literary & Artistic African-American Themes*. Available online at http://www.nathanielturner.com/howardthurman.htm.

ADAM CLAYTON POWELL JR.

1. Jim Haskins, *Adam Clayton Powell: Portrait of a Marching Black*. Trenton, NJ: Africa World Press reprint edition, 1993, p. 23.

2. Ibid., p. 114.

JOSEPH E. LOWERY

1. Black Leadership Forum website, http://www.blackleadershipforum.org/.

2. Online NewsHour: Farewell to Coretta Scott King—February 7, 2006. www.pbs.org/newshour/bb/remember/jan-june06/king_2-07.html.

MARTIN LUTHER KING JR.

1. James Haskins, *The Life and Death of Martin Luther King Jr.* New York: Lothrop, Lee & Shepard Co., 1977, p. 82.

ANDREW J. YOUNG

1. James Haskins, *Andrew Young: Man with a Mission.* New York: Lothrop, Lee & Shepard Co., 1979, p. 96.

2. Ibid., p. 145.

JOHN LEWIS

1. John Lewis, with Michael D'Orso, *Walking with the Wind: A Memoir of the Civil Rights Movement*. New York: Simon and Schuster, 1998, p. 77.

2. Ibid., p. 339.

3. Op. cit.

PRATHIA HALL WYNN

1. "Prathia Hall: A Lifetime of Speaking Out," *InSpire*, Summer 1998. Available online at http://www.ptsem.edu/Publications/inspire2/3.3/outstanding.htm.

2. Ibid.

FREDERICK J. STREETS

1. "A Conversation with Rev. Dr. Frederick J. Streets, University Chaplain and Senior Pastor of the Church of Christ, Yale University. February 2, 1999," The Gilder Lehrman Center for the Study of Slavery, Resistance, and Abolition. Available online at http://www.yale.edu/glc/archive/1023.htm.

AL SHARPTON

1. Al Sharpton and Anthony Walton, *Go and Tell Pharaoh: The Autobiography of the Reverend Al Sharpton.* New York: Doubleday & Co., 1996, p. 10.

2. Ibid., p. 23.

3. Ibid., p. 53.

4. Ibid., p. 232.

5. Ibid., back cover.

RENITA J. WEEMS

1. "Dry Spells and Philosophical Self-Doubt on the Spiritual Journey," *Virginian Pilot*, April 25, 1999, p. J2.

2. Ibid.

T. D. JAKES

1. Shayne Lee, *T. D. Jakes: America's New Preacher*. New York: New York University Press, 2005, p. 17.

2. Ibid., p. 58.

BIBLIOGRAPHY

BOOKS

Brown, William Wells. *The Black Man, His Antecedents, His Genius, and His Achievements*. Electronic edition: Documenting the American South, University of North Carolina, Chapel Hill, http://docsouth.unc.edu/neh/brownw/menu.html.

Frazier, E. Franklin, and C. Eric Lincoln. *The Negro Church in America/The Black Church Since Frazier*. New York: Schocken Books, 1974.

Harris, Frederick C. *Something Within: Religion in African-American Political Activism*. New York: Oxford University Press, 2001.

Haskins, Jim. *Jesse Jackson: Civil Rights Activist*. Berkeley Heights, NJ: Enslow Publishers, 2000.

———. *Louis Farrakhan and the Nation of Islam*. New York: Walker Books, 1996.

Henretta, James A., Elliot Brownlee, David Brody, Susan Ware, and Marilynn Johnson. *America's History*, 3rd ed. Worth Publishers Inc., 1997.

Lee, Jarena. *Religious Experience and Journal of Mrs. Jarena Lee Giving an Account of Her Call to Preach the Gospel*. Philadelphia, 1849. Electronic edition: http://onlinebooks .library.upenn.edu/webbin/book/lookupid?key=olbp21924.

Marrant, John. *A Narrative of the Lord's Wonderful Dealings with John Marrant, a Black (now going to preach the gospel in Nova-Scotia) . . . [Text from] Psalm 110:3 and Psalm 96:3. Fourth Edition, Enlarged by Mr. Marrant, and Printed (with permission) for His Sole Benefit, with Notes Explanatory* (printed for the author by R. Hawes, No. 40, Dorset-Street, Spitalfields, 1785). Available online at http://collections.ic.qc.ca/blackloyalists/people/religious/ marrant.htm.

Mayer, Henry. *All on Fire: William Lloyd Garrison and the Abolition of Slavery*. New York: St. Martin's Press, 1998.

Montgomery, William E. *Under Their Own Vine and Fig Tree: The African-American Church in the South, 1865–1900*. Baton Rouge: Louisiana State University, 1993.

Ponton, M. M. *Life and Times of Henry M. Turner; the Antecedent and Preliminary History of the Life and Times of Bishop H. M. Turner, His Boyhood, Education and Public Career, and His Relation to His Associates, Colleagues and Contemporaries*. New York: Negro Universities Press, 1970.

Raboteau, Albert J. *Slave Religion: The "Invisible Institution" in the Antebellum South*. New York: Oxford University Press, 1978.

Streets, Frederick J. *Preaching in the New Millennium: Celebrating the Tricentennial of Yale University*. New Haven, CT: Yale University Press, 2005.

Weems, The Reverend Renita J. *Listening for God: A Minister's Journey Through Silence and Doubt*. New York: Simon & Schuster Touchstone, 1999.

ARTICLES

"Black Chaplain Leaves Streets, Heads to Yale." *Albany Times Union*, May 23, 1992, p. B4.

Bogin, Ruth. "The Battle of Lexington: A Patriotic Ballad by Lemuel Haynes," *William and Mary Quarterly*, 3rd Ser., Vol. 42, No. 4 (Oct., 1985), pp. 499–506.

"Dry Spells and Philosophical Self-Doubt on the Spiritual Journey" (review). *Virginian Pilot*, April 25, 1999.

Freeburg, Christopher C. "Imagining Grace: Liberating Theologies in the Slave Narrative Tradition" (review). *American Literature*, Vol. 74, No. 3 (Sept. 2002).

Homewood, Glenn Small. "Sleuthing Prof Debunks Slave Plot." *Gazette Online, the Newspaper of Johns Hopkins University*, Vol. 31, No. 8 (Oct. 22, 2001).

Kinnon, Joy Bennett. "Spreading 'the Word' on Campus: African-American Chaplains Take the Lead in the Ivy League." *Ebony*, October 1, 2005.

May, Cedrick. "John Marrant, America's First Black Preacher." *African American Review*, Winter 2004.

———. "John Marrant and the Narrative Construction of an Early Black Methodist Evangelical." *Black History Review*, Winter 2004.

Railey, John. "Yale Chaplain Recounts His Road to the Ministry," *Winston-Salem Journal*, March 28, 2001.

Weiner, Jon. "Denmark Vesey: A New Verdict." *The Nation*, March 11, 2002. Available online at http://findarticles.com/p/articles/mi_hb1367/is_200203/ai_n5575257.

"Yale Names Baptist Pastor as Chaplain." *New York Times*, April 23, 1992.

OTHER SOURCES

A.J. and R.A. (Absalom Jones and Richard Allen). *A Narrative of the Proceedings of the Black People, During the Late Awful Calamity in Philadelphia, in the Year 1793; and A Refutation of Some Censures, Thrown upon Them in Some Late Publications*. Philadelphia, 1794. Available online at http://www.geocities.com/bobarnebeck/allen.html.

Burden, Jean. *"Howard Thurman,"* Chicken Bones: A Journal for Literary & Artistic African-American Themes. Available online at http://www.nathanielturner.com/howardthurman.htm.

"A Conversation with Rev. Dr. Frederick J. Streets, University Chaplain and Senior Pastor of the Church of Christ, Yale University. February 2, 1999." The Gilder Lehrman Center for the Study of Slavery, Resistance, and Abolition. Available online at http://www.yale.edu/glc/archive/1023.htm.

Hatcher, William E. *John Jasper: The Unmatched Negro Philosopher and Preacher*. New York: Fleming H. Revell Company, 1908, p. 75. Electronic edition: Documenting the American South, University of North Carolina, http://docsouth.unc.edu/church/hatcher/menu.html.

This Far by Faith: African-American Spiritual Journeys, a coproduction of Blackside Inc. and The Faith Project, Inc., in association with the Independent Television Service, presented on PBS by WGBH and ITVS

Walker, David. *Walker's Appeal, in Four Articles; Together with a Preamble, to the Coloured Citizens of the World, But in Particular, and Very Expressly, to Those of the United States of America, Written in Boston, State of Massachusetts, September 28, 1829*. Boston: David Walker, 1830. Electronic edition: Documenting the American South, University of North Carolina, http://docsouth.unc.edu/nc/walker/ menu.html.

PICTURE CREDITS

Page 7: Absalom Jones, 1810, Raphaelle Peale (1774–1825), Oil on p___r mounted to board. Courtesy of the Delaware Art Museum, Gift of Absalom ___es School, 1971. Richard Allen, 1784. Courtesy of the Moorland-Spingarn R___arch Center, Howard University; page 13: Jarena Lee, 1844. Courtesy of Lib___ of Congress, Prints and Photographs, LC-USZ62-42044; page 14: courtesy ___e Library of Congress, Prints and Photographs, LC-USZ62-42043; page ___ter Williams Sr., from the collection of the New-York Historical Society, As___ on No. X.173.; Peter Williams Jr. , Used with Permission of Documenting the ___rican South, The University of North Carolina at Chapel Hill Libraries;___ 17: drawing of John Marrant © 2007 by Michelle Whelan; page 27: courte___ the Library of Congress, Prints and Photographs, LC-DIG-ppmsca-08978; p___ ___: Nat Turner, American slave leader, steel engraving, 1863, after Felix O. C___rley, "Slave Rebellion"(Work Order W107312), courtesy of the Granger Collec___, New York; page 39: Maria Stewart, *Slavery: Woman*, 1832. Am I not a Wom___ ___nd a Sister?: American type-founder's cut, 1832 (Work Order W107313), c___esy of the Granger Collection, New York; page 42: from http://docsouth.u___.du/neh/jasper/randofp.jpg, used with permission of Documenting the Ame___n South, The University of North Carolina at Chapel Hill Libraries; page 48___exander Crummell, courtesy of the Photographs and Prints Division, Schor___rg Center for Research in Black Culture, The New York Public Library___tor, Lenox & Tilden Foundations; Henry Highland Garnett, courtesy of Gene___ ___esearch and Reference Division, Schomburg Center for Research in ___ck Culture, The New York Public Library, Astor, Lenox & Tilden Foundatio___ page 57: Henry McNeal Turner, courtesy of the Georgia Capitol Museum, C___ ___e of Secretary of State; page 62: from E. C. Morris, *Sermons, Addresses an___ ___miniscences and Important Correspondence*, Arno Press, 1980, Reprint edition;___ge 65: © Corbis; page 67: courtesy of the Oberlin College Archives, Oberlin, ___io; page 68: courtesy of the Library of Congress, Prints and Photographs, ___-DIG-fsa-8a26761; page 71: © Bettmann/Corbis; page 78: Used by permission ___ ___he Howard Thurman Estate. Photo from the Thurman Family Archives, and I___ ___pirit Communications and Film; page 85: courtesy of the Library of Congress, P___ts and Photographs, LC-USZ62-38826; page 91: courtesy of Joseph E. Lowery. ___ ___ed by permission; page 94: © Michael Ochs Archives/Corbis; p___ ___ 98: courtesy of the Library of Congress, Prints and Photographs, LC-U___ ___11696-9A; page 103: courtesy of the Library of Congress, Prints and Photo___ ___phs, LC-U9-34630A-13A; page 109 © Bettmann/Corbis; page 112: courtesy of ___ ___n Lewis; page 120 © Bettmann/Corbis; page 125 by John Chiasson. Used ___ ___ permission; page 131: courtesy of Dr. Frederick Jerry Streets. Used by perm___ ___ion; page 136: © Mark Peterson/Corbis; page 142: courtesy of Rev. Dr. Renita J. ___ ___ems, Ph.D. Used with permission; page 146: Thomas Michael Alleman/L___ ___on/Getty Images.

INDEX